What People Are Saying about Threshold Bible Study

"Stephen Binz's Threshold Bible Study is a marvelous project. With lucidity and creativity, Binz offers today's believing communities a rich and accessible treasury of biblical scholarship. The series' brilliance lies in its simplicity of presentation complemented by critical depth of thought and reflective insight. This is a wonderful gift for personal and communal study, especially for those wishing to make a home for the Word in their hearts."

Carol J. Dempsey, OP, Associate Professor of Theology, University of Portland, OR

"Threshold Bible Study successfully bridges the painful gap between solid biblical scholarship and the rich spiritual nourishment that we expect to find in the words of Scripture. In this way, indispensable biblical knowledge leads to that spiritual wisdom which enables us to live in accord with God's purposes. Stephen Binz is to be congratulated for responding to this urgent need in today's world."

Demetrius Dumm, O.S.B., Professor of New Testament, Saint Vincent Seminary, Saint Vincent Archabbey, Latrobe, Pennsylvania

"Threshold Bible Study provides an introduction to some major biblical themes, enabling Catholics to read, with greater understanding, the Bible in the Church. When studied along with the documents of Vatican II and the Catechism of the Catholic Church, this series can be a help for personal and group Bible study."

Francis Cardinal George, O.M.I., Archbishop of Chicago

"The Church has called Scripture a 'font' and 'wellspring' for the spiritual life. Threshold Bible Study is one of the best sources for tapping into the biblical font. Pope John Paul II has stressed that 'listening to the Word of God should become a life-giving encounter.' This is precisely what Threshold Bible Study offers to you—an encounter with the Word that will make your heart come alive."   Tim Gray, Director of the Denver Catholic Biblical School

"Threshold Bible Study is appropriately named, for its commentary and study questions bring people to the threshold of the text and invite them in. The questions guide but do not dominate. They lead readers to ponder and wrestle with the biblical passages and take them across the threshold toward life with God. Stephen Binz's work stands in the tradition of the biblical renewal movement and brings it back to life. We need more of this in the Church."

Kathleen M. O'Connor, Professor of Old Testament, Columbia Theological Seminary

"I most strongly recommend Stephen Binz's Threshold Bible Study for adult Bible classes, religious education, and personal spiritual enrichment. The series is exceptional for its scholarly solidity, pastoral practicality, and clarity of presentation. The church owes Binz a great debt of gratitude for his generous and competent labor in the service of the Word of God."
Peter C. Phan, The Ignacio Ellacuria Professor of Catholic Social Thought,
Georgetown University

"Threshold Bible Study is the perfect series of Bible study books for serious students with limited time. Each lesson is brief, illuminating, challenging, wittily written, and a pleasure to study. The reader will reap a rich harvest of wisdom from the efforts expended."
John J. Pilch, Adjunct Professor of Biblical Studies,
Georgetown University, Washington, DC

"I am please to endorse the Threshold Bible Study series. The thematic books are informative, easy to use, rooted in the Church's tradition of reflection and prayer, and of sound catechetical method."
Most Reverend Anthony M. Pilla, Bishop of Cleveland

"Threshold Bible Study helpfully introduces the lay reader into the life-enhancing process of Lectio Divina or prayerful reading of scripture, individually or in a group. This series, prepared by a reputable biblical scholar and teacher, responds creatively to the exhortation of the Council to provide God' people abundant nourishment from the table of God's word. The process proposed leads the reader from Bible study to personal prayer, community involvement, and active Christian commitment in the world."
Sandra M. Schneiders, Professor of New Testament and Spirituality,
Jesuit School of Theology, Berkeley

"Threshold Bible Study unlocks the Scriptures and ushers the reader over the threshold into the world of God's living Word. The world of the Bible comes alive with new meaning and understanding for our times. This series enables the reader to appreciate contemporary biblical scholarship and the meaning of God's Word. This is the best material I have seen for serious Bible study."
Most Reverend Donald W. Trautman, Bishop of Erie

"Threshold Bible Study is that rare kind of program that will help one cross an elusive threshold—using the Bible effectively for prayer and spiritual enrichment. This user-friendly program will enhance any personal or group Bible study. Guaranteed to make your love of Scripture grow!"
Ronald D. Witherup, S.S., biblical scholar and author of *The Bible Companion*

The TRAGIC and TRIUMPHANT CROSS

Stephen J. Binz

TWENTY
THIRD *23rd*
PUBLICATIONS

Fourth printing 2011

TWENTY-THIRD PUBLICATIONS
A Division of Bayard
One Montauk Avenue, Suite 200
New London, CT 06320
(860) 437-3012 or (800) 321-0411
www.23rdpublications.com

The Scripture passages contained herein are from the *New Revised Standard Version of the Bible*, Catholic edition. Copyright ©1989, by the Division of Christian Education of the National Council of Churches in the U.S.A. All rights reserved.

ISBN: 978-1-58595-317-2
Library of Congress Catalog Card Number: 2004114737
Printed in the U.S.A.

Contents

How to Use
Threshold Bible Study

Each book in the Threshold Bible Study series is designed to lead you through a new doorway of biblical awareness, to accompany you across a unique threshold of understanding. The characters, places, and images that you encounter in each of these topical studies will help you explore fresh dimensions of your faith and discover richer insights for your spiritual life.

Threshold Bible Study covers biblical themes in depth in a short amount of time. Unlike more traditional Bible studies that treat a biblical book or series of books, Threshold Bible Study aims to address specific topics within the entire Bible. The goal is not for you to comprehend everything about each passage, but rather for you to understand what a variety of passages from different books of the Bible reveals about the topic of each study.

Threshold Bible Study offers you an opportunity to explore the entire Bible from the viewpoint of a variety of different themes. The commentary that follows each biblical passage launches your reflection about that passage and helps you begin to see its significance within the context of your contemporary experience. The questions following the commentary challenge you to understand the passage more fully and apply it to your own life. The prayer starter helps conclude your study by integrating learning into your relationship with God.

These studies are designed for maximum flexibility. Each study is presented in a workbook format, with sections for reading, reflecting, writing, discussing, and praying. Space for writing after each question is ideal for personal study and allows group members to prepare in advance for their discussion. The thirty lessons in each topic may be used by an individual over the period of a month, or by a group for six sessions, with lessons to be studies each week before the next group meeting. These studies are ideal for Bible study groups, small Christian communities, adult faith formation, student groups, Sunday school, neighborhood groups, and family reading, as well as for individual learning.

The method of Threshold Bible Study is rooted in the classical tradition of *lectio divina*, an ancient yet contemporary means for reading the Scriptures reflectively and prayerfully. Reading and interpreting the text (*lectio*) is followed by reflective meditation on its message (*meditatio*). This reading and reflecting flows into prayer from the heart (*oratio* and *contemplatio*).

This ancient method assures us that Bible study is a matter of both the mind and the heart. It is not just an intellectual exercise to learn more and be able to discuss the Bible with others. It is, more importantly, a transforming experience. Reflecting on God's word, guided by the Holy Spirit, illumines the mind with wisdom and stirs the heart with zeal.

Following the personal Bible study, Threshold Bible Study offers a method for extending *lectio divina* into a weekly conversation with a small group. This communal experience will allow participants to enhance their appreciation of the message and build up a spiritual community (*collatio*). The end result will be to increase not only individual faith, but also faithful witness in the context of daily life (*operatio*).

Through the spiritual disciplines of Scripture reading, study, reflection, conversation, and prayer, you will experience God's grace more abundantly as your life is rooted more deeply in Christ. The risen Jesus said: "Listen! I am standing at the door, knocking; if you hear my voice and open the door, I will come in to you and eat with you, and you with me" (Rev 3:20). Listen to the Word of God, open the door, and cross the threshold to an unimaginable dwelling with God!

SUGGESTIONS FOR INDIVIDUAL STUDY

• Make your Bible reading a time of prayer. Ask for God's guidance as you read the Scriptures.

• Try to study daily, or as often as possible according to the circumstances of your life.

• Read the Bible passage carefully, trying to understand both its meaning and its personal application as you read. Some persons find it helpful to read the passage aloud.

• Read the passage in another Bible translation. Each version adds to your understanding of the original text.

• Allow the commentary to help you comprehend and apply the scriptural text. The commentary is only a beginning, not the last word on the meaning of the passage.

• After reflecting on each question, write out your responses. The very act of writing will help you clarify your thoughts, bring new insights, and amplify your understanding.

• As you reflect on your answers, think about how you can live God's word in the context of your daily life.

• Conclude each daily lesson by reading the prayer and continuing with your own prayer from the heart.

• Make sure your reflections and prayers are matters of both the mind and the heart. A true encounter with God's word is always a transforming experience.

• Choose a word or a phrase from the lesson to carry with you throughout the day as a reminder of your encounter with God's life-changing word.

• Share your learning experience with at least one other person whom you trust for additional insights and affirmation. The ideal way to share learning is in a small group that meets regularly.

SUGGESTIONS FOR GROUP STUDY

• Meet regularly; weekly is ideal. Try to be on time and make attendance a high priority for the sake of the group. The average group meets for about an hour.

• Open each session with a prepared prayer, a song, or a reflection. Find some appropriate way to bring the group from the workaday world into a sacred time of graced sharing.

• If you have not been together before, name tags are very helpful as a group begins to become acquainted with the other group members.

• Spend the first session getting acquainted with one another, reading the Introduction aloud, and discussing the questions that follow.

• Appoint a group facilitator to provide guidance to the discussion. The role of facilitator may rotate among members each week. The facilitator simply keeps the discussion on track; each person shares responsibility for the group. There is no need for the facilitator to be a trained teacher.

• Try to study the six lessons on your own during the week. When you have done your own reflection and written your own answers, you will be better prepared to discuss the six scriptural lessons with the group. If you have not had an opportunity to study the passages during the week, meet with the group anyway to share support and insights.

• Participate in the discussion as much as you are able, offering your thoughts, insights, feelings, and decisions. You learn by sharing with others the fruits of your study.

• Be careful not to dominate the discussion. It is important that everyone in the group be offered an equal opportunity to share the results of their work. Try to link what you say to the comments of others so that the group remains on the topic.

• When discussing your own personal thoughts or feelings, use "I" language. Be as personal and honest as appropriate and be very cautious about giving advice to others.

• Listen attentively to the other members of the group so as to learn from their insights. The words of the Bible affect each person in a different way, so a group provides a wealth of understanding for each member.

• Don't fear silence. Silence in a group is as important as silence in personal study. It allows individuals time to listen to the voice of God's Spirit and the opportunity to form their thoughts before they speak.

• Solicit several responses for each question. The thoughts of different people will build on the answers of others and will lead to deeper insights for all.

• Don't fear controversy. Differences of opinions are a sign of a healthy and honest group. If you cannot resolve an issue, continue on, agreeing to disagree. There is probably some truth in each viewpoint.

• Discuss the questions that seem most important for the group. There is no need to cover all the questions in the group session.

• Realize that some questions about the Bible cannot be resolved, even by experts. Don't get stuck on some issue for which there are no clear answers.

• Whatever is said in the group is said in confidence and should be regarded as such.

• Pray as a group in whatever way feels comfortable. Pray for the members of your group throughout the week.

Schedule for group study

Session 1: Introduction   Date _____

Session 2: Lessons 1-6   Date _____

Session 3: Lessons 7-12   Date _____

Session 4: Lessons 13-18   Date _____

Session 5: Lessons 19-24   Date _____

Session 6: Lessons 25-30   Date _____

He humbled himself and became obedient to the point of death
—even death on a cross.
Phil 2:8

The Tragic and Triumphant Cross

The cross stands at the very heart of the Christian faith. It is Christianity's most important and powerful symbol. Like all true symbols, it evokes more than can be explained in words and contains multiple levels of meaning. The cross reminds us of the suffering and death of Jesus; it also reminds us of his victory over death and his glorious, risen life. The cross is the world's most hated instrument of torture, the most horrible form of punishment. It expresses some of humanity's deepest fears: pain, betrayal, abandonment, death. Yet, the cross is also the symbol of humanity's greatest hope—that suffering and death do not have the last word, that life does arise from death, that God is trustworthy.

The power of the sign of the cross is nowhere more beautifully expressed than in the ritual for receiving candidates into the catechumenate—the Rite of Acceptance—to begin their preparation for baptism. In some parishes, the candidates are asked to place their hands on a large wooden cross as a sign of their acceptance of the cross of Christ. The presider prays for each candidate by name while tracing the cross on the candidate's forehead: "Receive the

1

cross on your forehead. It is Christ himself who now strengthens you with this sign of love. Learn to know him and follow him."

The sponsors of the candidates then trace the cross over the candidate's ears, eyes, lips, breast, shoulders, hands, and feet:

> Receive the sign of the cross on your ears,
> that you may hear the voice of the Lord.
> Receive the sign of the cross on your eyes,
> that you may see the glory of God.
> Receive the sign of the cross on your lips,
> that you may respond to the word of God.
> Receive the sign of the cross over your heart,
> that Christ may dwell there by faith.
> Receive the sign of the cross on your shoulders,
> that you may bear the gentle yoke of Christ.
> Receive the sign of the cross on your hands,
> that Christ may be known in the work which you do.
> Receive the sign of the cross on your feet,
> that you may walk in the way of Christ.

This practice of signing with the cross continues throughout the life of the baptized. Following an ancient practice, we trace the cross on our forehead, lips, and heart as we prepare to hear the Gospel proclaimed. Catholic and Orthodox Christians make the sign of the cross at the beginning of liturgy or prayer, a dramatic gesture tracing the cross over the whole body. Sometimes parents trace the cross on the forehead of their children as they put them to bed each night. Truly, the followers of Jesus are marked with the cross, the symbol that expresses most explicitly who we are.

Reflection and discussion

• What is my favorite image of the cross? What is its particular meaning for me?

• What message do I proclaim when I wear a cross on my neck or hang a crucifix in my home?

In the country of Lithuania, there is a pilgrimage site called the Hill of Crosses. Here hundreds of thousands of crosses, of all sizes and descriptions, are spiked into its sacred ground. Pilgrims come to this hill from every corner of the country, carrying their crosses, desiring to leave a memorial to their pain, to express a heart-felt need, or to offer thanks for a recent blessing. Some crosses are painstakingly carved, others are crude and bare; some hold images of Christ or the Virgin Mary, others hold pictures of loved ones who died during the Nazi occupation, who were deported to Siberia, or who suffered and died under the sign of the cross.

This hill is called the soul of Lithuania, a vivid relic of its past, a reminder of its cruel and glorious history. The hill was bulldozed over and over again during the Soviet occupation, out of disdain for the "ignorance and fanaticism" that it represented to them. But no force could prevent the faithful from returning at night to start over again. The Hill of Crosses is a powerful symbol of resistance to occupation and oppression, an enduring sign of strength and hope.

The cross is planted on mountaintops around the world and displayed on the walls of Christian homes. It is mounted on church tops and dangled around the necks of disciples. We find rugged wooden crosses and ornately jeweled crosses, images of the suffering Christ and images of the risen Christ affixed to the cross. The symbol of the cross has the power to galvanize the followers of Jesus. In processions and liturgies, in poetry and music, in architecture and devotions, the cross speaks to what we believe about Jesus and about how we understand our lives in relationship to him. It is the primordial symbol by which we express our commitment to Christ and through which we experience the love of God.

Reflection and discussion

• Why is the cross the central symbol and universal expression of Christianity?

• What personal experiences have helped me gain a deeper understanding of the meaning of Christ's cross?

After so many centuries in which the cross has been revered as a sacred symbol, it is difficult for us to imagine the utter horror and revulsion that even the mention of the cross provoked in the ancient world. Crucifixion was not simply an early form of capital punishment, comparable to our electric chair, gas chamber, or lethal injection. The Jewish historian Josephus called it "the most wretched of deaths." In Roman society the Latin word crux (cross) was considered an obscene, four-letter word, not to be uttered in polite conversation. Crucifixion was, by intent, cruel and unusual punishment, used by the Romans to inspire terror in those who witnessed death on a cross. More than any other suffering, crucifixion manifested the extremes of inhuman cruelty.

Yet, through bearing this contemptible form of punishment, Jesus produced the most dramatic reversal the world has ever experienced. He turned this instrument of torture into the object of his followers' proudest boast: "May I never boast of anything," said Paul," except the cross of our Lord Jesus Christ" (Gal 6:14).

The passion and death of Jesus on the cross was the heart of the earliest Christian proclamation and the center of Christian belief. Paul taught that Jesus humbled himself, becoming like a slave, obedient unto death, "even death on a cross" (Phil 2:8). His death was "foolishness" in the eyes of the world, a "stumbling-block" for many, yet in God's design "wisdom" and "power" (1 Cor 1:18, 23-24). The gospels reach their climax in the passion accounts. In the gospel of Mark, the question "Who do you say I am?" is answered most fully at the death of Jesus on the cross: "Truly this man was the Son of God" (Mark 15:39).

In every age it is tempting to deny the full reality of the cross. We like serene crucifixes. The gospel could be made much more intellectually and emotionally attractive if we suppressed its most distinctive feature—the crucifixion of Jesus. Every age of Christianity is tempted to explain salvation in a way that can be defended by logical argument and will not make us look foolish—in a way that denies the full reality of the cross. Plain and simple, the cross is a scandal. We must not deny its scandalous nature so that, as Paul says, "the cross of Christ might not be emptied of its power" (1 Cor 1:17).

A God who remained isolated from human suffering, majestically insulated in his heaven, would not be a convincing or reliable God in our suffering world. The cross is our most powerful reminder that God is with us even in pain and tragedy and seemingly hopeless situations. Paul gave meaning to his own suffering by considering suffering an opportunity to be united in the love that Jesus showed in his death on the cross: "always carrying in the body the death of Jesus, so that the life of Jesus may also be made visible in our bodies" (2 Cor 4:10). Paul said that his own wounds are "the marks of Jesus" on his body (Gal 6:17). Though suffering is often senseless and irrational, we do not suffer alone. Such realization allows us to endure and accept the suffering that is part of our human condition and the pain that comes in every life.

Reflection and discussion

• Why are we tempted to deny the full reality of the cross?

• In his life for us, Christ has plunged into the depth of every human experience. What comfort or hope does this truth offer me?

Often human suffering is not inevitable or irrational; it is the result of human sinfulness. People are oppressed by others and by human systems that prevent them from living with dignity. The cross is a symbol of resistance to this type of suffering. The cross empowers Christians to resist evil, rather than be complicit in it. Our task is not to mirror our culture but to convert it, and the cross calls us to do just that in the most radical of ways. The folk art of Central America depicts scenes of joyful life and simple abundance painted on the form of the cross. It is a wonderful expression of human resistance in the midst of oppression, of the choice to live abundantly despite life's hardships, of hope that suffering will be transformed.

For Jesus, the cross was not just his final act; it expressed his entire life of sacrifice for others, of laying down his life out of love. The life of a disciple is described by Jesus as following in his way: "If any want to become my followers, let them deny themselves and take up their cross and follow me" (Mark 8:34). For us, the cross is the symbol that pouring out our lives for another brings new life when we do it in imitation of Jesus. In every age and in every place the followers of Jesus must choose between the way of the crowd and the way of the cross. The call to follow Jesus in service of all kinds is always shaped by the cross.

Reflection and discussion

• In what way is the cross counter-cultural today?

• Why is it necessary to express the message of the cross anew in every generation?

T his study invites us to stand at the foot of the cross and to gaze on it through the eyes of the various biblical writers. The writings of the gospels, selected Old Testament texts, and the letters of Paul and others will help us reflect on the meaning of the cross and gradually probe its mystery. No single interpretation of the cross is adequate to explain it all. The cross is a sign that is both tragic and triumphant, a call to persevere in the way of suffering and a power that offers renewal and hope.

The logic of the cross seems to fly in the face of common sense. Why is suffering and death the way to life? Why is the dreaded cross our clearest sign of hope? Why is this instrument of torture the universal symbol that inspires more people than any other? What does the call of Jesus to take up the cross imply for my life? The cross is a great paradox: we will never fully understand it. The tragedy outside the walls of Jerusalem in A.D. 30 was God's triumph over sin, death, and meaningless existence. This is the great mystery that we will seek to unravel as we study the tragic and triumphant cross.

Prayer

Crucified Lord, there is no depth of human experience to which you have not plunged. You know the darkness of fear, the loneliness of suffering, the dread of depression, and the agony of death. You entered fully into the intensity of human pain and transformed it by your love. Through your holy cross, you have brought light out of darkness, life out of death, and you have redeemed the world. As I reflect on the great mystery of your cross, teach me to be a cross-bearing disciple so that I can extend your love to the world.

SUGGESTIONS FOR FACILITATORS, GROUP SESSION 1

1. If the group is meeting for the first time, or if there are newcomers joining the group, it is helpful to provide nametags.

2. Ask the participants to introduce themselves and tell the group a bit about themselves. You may want to ask one or more of these introductory questions:
   • What is your biggest fear in beginning this Bible study?
   • How is beginning this study like a "threshold" for you?

3. Distribute the books to the members of the group.

4. Display a cross or crucifix during this and future sessions. You may want to light a candle to be kept burning throughout the discussion and prayer.

5. You may want to pray this prayer as a group:
Come upon us, Holy Spirit, to enlighten and guide us as we begin this study of the tragic and triumphant cross. You inspired the writers of the Scriptures to reveal the message of the cross in many different ways throughout the history of salvation. Now stir our minds and our hearts to penetrate the mystery of the cross and to proclaim that cross as the sign of good news for all people. Motivate us to read the Scriptures, give us a love for God's word, and help us to learn the way of discipleship through this study of Christ's cross. Bless us during this session and throughout the coming week with the fire of your love.

6. Read the Introduction aloud, pausing at each question for discussion. Group members may wish to write the insights of the group as each question is discussed. Encourage several members of the group to respond to each question.

7. Don't feel compelled to finish the complete Introduction during the session. It is better to allow sufficient time to talk about the questions raised than to rush to the end. Group members may read any remaining sections on their own after the group meeting.

8. Instruct group members to read the first six lessons on their own during the six days before the next group meeting. They should write out their own answers to the questions as preparation for next week's group discussion.

9. Fill in the date for each group meeting under "Schedule for Group Study."

10. Conclude by praying aloud together the prayer at the end of the Introduction.

"If any want to become my followers, let them deny themselves and take up their cross and follow me." Mark 8:34

Cross-Bearing Discipleship

MARK 8:29-38 ²⁹*[Jesus] asked them, "But who do you say that I am?" Peter answered him, "You are the Messiah." ³⁰And he sternly ordered them not to tell anyone about him.*

³¹Then he began to teach them that the Son of Man must undergo great suffering, and be rejected by the elders, the chief priests, and the scribes, and be killed, and after three days rise again. ³²He said all this quite openly. And Peter took him aside and began to rebuke him. ³³But turning and looking at his disciples, he rebuked Peter and said, "Get behind me, Satan! For you are setting your mind not on divine things but on human things."

³⁴He called the crowd with his disciples, and said to them, "If any want to become my followers, let them deny themselves and take up their cross and follow me. ³⁵For those who want to save their life will lose it, and those who lose their life for my sake, and for the sake of the gospel, will save it. ³⁶For what will it profit them to gain the whole world and forfeit their life? ³⁷Indeed, what can they give in return for their life? ³⁸Those who are ashamed of me and of my words in this adulterous and sinful generation, of them the Son of Man will also be ashamed when he comes in the glory of his Father with the holy angels."

The shadow of the cross casts itself over the entire gospel. From beginning to end, the gospel of Mark is the good news of Jesus the Crucified One. This passage is found at the midpoint of the gospel. Peter answers the crucial question of Jesus and confesses Jesus to be the Messiah (verse 29). Then Jesus gives the first of three explicit predictions of his own suffering, leading up to the passion account. Jesus sets his face toward the cross, as the goal and destiny of his mission.

Peter was unable to accept the idea that Jesus the Messiah would have to suffer, and the idea of being a disciple of a suffering Messiah did not appeal to him. So Peter took Jesus aside and began to chastise him, presumably trying to get Jesus to conform to the popularly accepted notion of a Messiah who would enjoy worldly triumph (verse 32). Then Jesus rebuked Peter, accusing him of taking the role of Satan, the one who was trying to turn Jesus away from God's will and saving purpose.

After the prediction of his passion, Jesus describes the life of a disciple. He asks his followers not only to believe in his message, but to attach themselves to him and walk in his path. Those who wish to follow Jesus must do three things (verse 34). First, disciples must deny themselves—not be preoccupied with their own interests. Second, disciples must take up their cross—patiently bearing trials and being prepared to sacrifice. Third, disciples must follow Jesus—accepting his way of life and imitating his generous self-giving.

When these three aspects of discipleship are understood together, it is clear that Jesus is asking his followers to make a radical choice. Mark's concern as the gospel writer is for the persecuted Christians of his own day. These sayings of Jesus remind them that following a rejected and crucified Messiah implies that they too will have to endure suffering. The way of the cross is not the way of the world. A true disciple must not be ashamed of Jesus' way of humiliation, suffering, and death (verse 38), but must be prepared to risk all for Jesus and his gospel. Disciples of Jesus are to be cross-bearers. The cross is not only something Jesus carried for them, but also something they carry for him and others. In some areas of our world today disciples still experience harassment, hostility, imprisonment, and even martyrdom. Even in tolerant countries, followers of Jesus often experience misunderstanding and antagonism. But all disciples are called to carry the cross, whether it be in the form of persecution or the self-giving love of anguish and grief.

Reflection and discussion

• What does it mean to say that the shadow of the cross casts itself over the entire gospel?

• Why was following a rejected and suffering Messiah so difficult for Peter?

• What three aspects of following Jesus are listed in verse 34? Which is most challenging for me?

Prayer

Crucified Jesus, you call me to deny myself, take up my cross, and follow you. Help me to accept a life of self-sacrifice and imitate your generosity. May I never be ashamed of your cross.

So Pilate released Barabbas for them; and after flogging Jesus, he handed him over to be crucified. Mark 15:15

"Crucify him!"

MARK 15:1-15 ¹*As soon as it was morning, the chief priests held a consultation with the elders and scribes and the whole council. They bound Jesus, led him away, and handed him over to Pilate.* ²*Pilate asked him, "Are you the King of the Jews?" He answered him, "You say so."* ³*Then the chief priests accused him of many things.* ⁴*Pilate asked him again, "Have you no answer? See how many charges they bring against you."* ⁵*But Jesus made no further reply, so that Pilate was amazed.*

⁶*Now at the festival he used to release a prisoner for them, anyone for whom they asked.* ⁷*Now a man called Barabbas was in prison with the rebels who had committed murder during the insurrection.* ⁸*So the crowd came and began to ask Pilate to do for them according to his custom.* ⁹*Then he answered them, "Do you want me to release for you the King of the Jews?"* ¹⁰*For he realized that it was out of jealousy that the chief priests had handed him over.* ¹¹*But the chief priests stirred up the crowd to have him release Barabbas for them instead.* ¹²*Pilate spoke to them again, "Then what do you wish me to do with the man you call the King of the Jews?"* ¹³*They shouted back, "Crucify him!"* ¹⁴*Pilate asked them, "Why, what evil has he done?" But they shouted all the more, "Crucify him!"* ¹⁵*So Pilate, wishing to satisfy the crowd, released Barabbas for them; and after flogging Jesus, he handed him over to be crucified.*

No other ancient biographies are so preoccupied with the death of their subject as are the gospels. Jesus' demise is clearly the most famous death in history. The end of his life has exercised an incomparable hold and fascination over the minds and imaginations of people of many cultures and eras. The gospel of Mark has been called a passion narrative with a long introduction. Everything leads to the cross of Jesus.

The nature of Jesus' identity as the suffering Messiah is illuminated as Jesus is sentenced to death and crucified. In response to Pilate's question, "Are you the king of the Jews?" Jesus answers ambiguously: "You say so" (verse 2). The title points to a fundamental truth about Jesus—he is indeed the royal Messiah—yet clearly neither Pilate nor the religious leaders understand how this man of sorrows could be a king.

Jesus is then accused of many things (verse 3), and Pilate is astonished that Jesus does not speak in his own defense (verse 5). Jesus will remain silent until his cry from the cross. He exemplifies the uncomplaining acceptance of the suffering servant found in the prophet Isaiah. Truly Jesus was "like a lamb that is led to the slaughter, and like a sheep that before its shearers is silent, so he did not open his mouth" (Isa 53:7).

It was a custom at the time of Passover, the feast of liberation, that a Jewish prisoner be freed. Assuming the people would want Jesus released, Pilate placed the fate of Jesus in the hands of the crowd. When Pilate asked what he should do with the man they called the king of the Jews, the crowd shouted, "Crucify him" (verse 13). The last time a crowd shouted in the gospel was at the entry of Jesus into Jerusalem, to the shouts of "Hosanna" (11:9). The sudden change in the crowd's response to Jesus, from praise to condemnation, is brutally shocking.

Pilate finally handed Jesus over to be crucified because he wanted to "satisfy the crowd" (verse 15). In choosing Barabbas, a rebel and murderer, the crowd demonstrates that they fail to understand the identity of Jesus. They join the cast of characters throughout the gospel who are scandalized that the Messiah should suffer, a scandal which is the heart of the contradiction called the cross. Truly we are all Barabbas—a name which literally means "son of the father." Jesus was crucified in our place. As he did for Barabbas, Jesus took our guilt upon himself, and let us go free.

Reflection and discussion

• How does the gospel demonstrate that many people are responsible for the crucifixion of Jesus? Why is it so wrong to blame only one group?

• How could the crowd who welcomed Jesus into Jerusalem now shout "Crucify him"? How do I feel when I cry "Crucify him" while reading the passion accounts?

• Imagine the reaction of Barabbas as he watched Jesus being condemned in place of himself. What might have been some of his thoughts and feelings?

Prayer

Innocent Jesus, you offered yourself so that I might live. Your cross unshackled the bonds of my captivity and set me free. Help me to give my life for others and to love as you have loved.

"Let the Messiah, the King of Israel, come down from the cross now, so that we may see and believe." Mark 15:32

The Crucified Messiah

MARK 15:16-32 ¹⁶*Then the soldiers led him into the courtyard of the palace (that is, the governor's headquarters); and they called together the whole cohort.* ¹⁷*And they clothed him in a purple cloak; and after twisting some thorns into a crown, they put it on him.* ¹⁸*And they began saluting him, "Hail, King of the Jews!"* ¹⁹*They struck his head with a reed, spat upon him, and knelt down in homage to him.* ²⁰*After mocking him, they stripped him of the purple cloak and put his own clothes on him. Then they led him out to crucify him.*

²¹*They compelled a passer-by, who was coming in from the country, to carry his cross; it was Simon of Cyrene, the father of Alexander and Rufus.* ²²*Then they brought Jesus to the place called Golgotha (which means the place of a skull).* ²³*And they offered him wine mixed with myrrh; but he did not take it.* ²⁴*And they crucified him, and divided his clothes among them, casting lots to decide what each should take.*

²⁵*It was nine o'clock in the morning when they crucified him.* ²⁶*The inscription of the charge against him read, "The King of the Jews."* ²⁷*And with him they crucified two bandits, one on his right and one on his left.* ²⁹*Those who passed by derided him, shaking their heads and saying, "Aha! You who would destroy the temple and build it in three days,* ³⁰*save yourself, and come down from the cross!"* ³¹*In the same way the chief priests, along with the scribes, were also mocking him*

among themselves and saying, "He saved others; he cannot save himself. [32] Let the Messiah, the King of Israel, come down from the cross now, so that we may see and believe." Those who were crucified with him also taunted him.

Six times in this chapter Jesus is spoken of as "king." The Roman soldiers mock Jesus' alleged claims to be king. They clothe him in mock royal garments and place a crown of thorns on his head (verse 17). With cruel violence they hail him as king, striking his head with a reed and spitting upon him (verses 18-19). The great irony of this bitter parody is that Jesus is really a king; yet he is not a king whose power and authority are displayed in worldly ways. What was spoken in bitter mockery and jest is actually true; he is a king of a most unexpected sort. Throughout his ministry Jesus had been demonstrating his sovereign power over hunger, sickness, demons, and even death. His ruling power reached its summit not by avoiding the cross but by accepting it.

Prisoners condemned to crucifixion were often made to carry their own cross, or at least the crossbeam. Apparently Jesus was already weakened by the torture he had endured. Simon, who must have come to Jerusalem for the Passover, was pressed into service to carry the cross of Jesus (verse 21). This man, who enters and exits the passion narrative in one verse, reminds us of the nature of discipleship. Taking up the cross was described by Jesus as the mark of true discipleship (8:34).

The place of execution is called Golgotha, which Mark translates for his readers as "place of a skull" (verse 22). The details of the crucifixion are stark: the soldiers offered him a narcotic which he refused (verse 23), they divided his garments by casting lots (verse 24), they inscribed his charge as "The King of the Jews" (verse 26), two others were crucified to his right and his left (verse 27).

This scene of horror, with Jesus affixed to the cross and his royal title fastened to the wood, is Mark's depiction of Jesus fully revealed as the suffering Messiah. The notion that a crucified king could be honored was strange indeed. There had been numerous messianic movements during the century in which Jesus lived, yet none of these would-be messiahs had any thought that their cause would come to fruition through his own death. Yet, in a profound sense, Jesus truly reigned from the cross and brought his kingdom into existence through it.

The crucified Jesus is cruelly mocked by those who pass by, the religious leaders, and those crucified with him. With supreme irony, the mockeries are expressions of Jesus' truest identity: the temple destroyed and rebuilt (verse

29), the one who saves others but not himself (verse 31), the one who remained on the cross so that others may believe (verse 32). His mission was accomplished in the most paradoxical form.

Reflection and discussion

• How does the passion show in the most unexpected ways that Jesus is a king?

• Who has been a Simon of Cyrene for me, helping me carry the cross? How can I be a Simon for others?

• How are the three cruel mockeries of Jesus on the cross expressions of his truest identity?

Prayer

Crucified Savior, you reign from the cross and establish your kingdom in pain. Help me trust that real power and victory is available through the weakness and humility of the cross.

Then Jesus gave a loud cry and breathed his last. Mark 15:37

A Brutal, Lonely Death

MARK 15:33-41 *³³When it was noon, darkness came over the whole land until three in the afternoon. ³⁴At three o'clock Jesus cried out with a loud voice, "Eloi, Eloi, lema sabachthani?" which means, "My God, my God, why have you forsaken me?" ³⁵When some of the bystanders heard it, they said, "Listen, he is calling for Elijah." ³⁶And someone ran, filled a sponge with sour wine, put it on a stick, and gave it to him to drink, saying, "Wait, let us see whether Elijah will come to take him down." ³⁷Then Jesus gave a loud cry and breathed his last. ³⁸And the curtain of the temple was torn in two, from top to bottom. ³⁹Now when the centurion, who stood facing him, saw that in this way he breathed his last, he said, "Truly this man was God's Son!"*

⁴⁰There were also women looking on from a distance; among them were Mary Magdalene, and Mary the mother of James the younger and of Joses, and Salome. ⁴¹These used to follow him and provided for him when he was in Galilee; and there were many other women who had come up with him to Jerusalem.

Mark's stark portrayal of the death of Jesus is the climax of his gospel. He gives no bitter details of the physical process of Jesus' death; his readers were all too familiar with the horrors of cruci-

18

fixion. Jesus has been abandoned by his disciples (14:50); he stood alone, in utter isolation. Was he now abandoned even by God? There was no light from heaven; darkness covered the land until his death (verse 33). The gloominess recalls the darkness that covered the land of Egypt before the first Passover (Exod 10:21-22) and the dreariness prophesied for the day of God's judgment: "I will make the sun go down at noon, and darken the earth in broad daylight" (Amos 8:9).

Jesus cried out the opening words of Psalm 22, "My God, my God, why have you forsaken me?" (verse 34), a tormented cry of one who has been abandoned. Jesus experienced no comfort; only God-forsakenness. Some commentators have tried to soften the scene and reduce its profound desolation. They have said that the opening words of Psalm 22 imply that Jesus prayed the entire psalm before his death, changing the final words of Jesus from a cry of abandonment to a prayer of trust. Yet it seems clear from Mark's stark presentation that Jesus felt abandoned by the Father with whom he had lived in intimate closeness, a suffering even worse than his shame, nakedness, and physical torture. At the moment in which Jesus most fully embodied God's love, he felt totally deserted by God. Why? Surely it is because Jesus totally took the sin of the world upon himself, a sin that separates us from God. He died the most bitter of all deaths in order to save us from such a fate.

With a loud and wordless cry, Jesus stopped breathing (verse 37). More than any other New Testament writing, the Gospel of Mark expresses the fierce brutality of Jesus' torturous death.

The first consequence of Jesus' death is the rending of the temple curtain (verse 38). The temple veil probably refers to the curtain that hung between the inner sanctuary and the Holy of Holies. The tearing from top to bottom symbolizes the new access to God which Christ's death won for all people. The second consequence of the death of Jesus is the confession of the Roman centurion as he watched Jesus die on the cross. His words are the fullest expression of Jesus' identity: "Truly this man was the Son of God!" (verse 39). Both of these consequences signify that on the cross Jesus has established a new, inclusive community of disciples. One of these new disciples is the Roman soldier, a Gentile, a man outside the community of Israel. With him also are the women, those faithful disciples who stood with Jesus at his cross when the others had fled. The tearing of the temple curtain in two dramatically underlines what the people at the foot of the cross express: the cross has made access to God available to all, regardless of race, status, or gender. From now on, the way to forgiveness and unity with God is through the cross.

Reflection and discussion

• When have I felt abandoned by God? How does the fact that Jesus truly felt abandoned by God help me?

• What do the two dramatic consequences of Jesus' death tell me about the effects of his death?

• Why does the gospel note that only the women stood with Jesus at the cross? What happened to the men?

Prayer

Lord Jesus, through your cross you have opened the way to God and gathered me into the community of your disciples. Thank you for remaining on the cross so that I may live.

At that moment the curtain of the temple was torn in two.
The earth shook, and the rocks were split. Matt 27:51

The Apocalyptic Crucifixion

MATTHEW 27:45–56 [45]*From noon on, darkness came over the whole land until three in the afternoon.* [46]*And about three o'clock Jesus cried with a loud voice, "Eli, Eli, lema sabachthani?" that is, "My God, my God, why have you forsaken me?"* [47]*When some of the bystanders heard it, they said, "This man is calling for Elijah."* [48]*At once one of them ran and got a sponge, filled it with sour wine, put it on a stick, and gave it to him to drink.* [49]*But the others said, "Wait, let us see whether Elijah will come to save him."* [50]*Then Jesus cried again with a loud voice and breathed his last.* [51]*At that moment the curtain of the temple was torn in two, from top to bottom. The earth shook, and the rocks were split.* [52]*The tombs also were opened, and many bodies of the saints who had fallen asleep were raised.* [53]*After his resurrection they came out of the tombs and entered the holy city and appeared to many.* [54]*Now when the centurion and those with him, who were keeping watch over Jesus, saw the earthquake and what took place, they were terrified and said, "Truly this man was God's Son!"*

[55]*Many women were also there, looking on from a distance; they had followed Jesus from Galilee and had provided for him.* [56]*Among them were Mary Magdalene, and Mary the mother of James and Joseph, and the mother of the sons of Zebedee.*

The passion accounts of the four Gospels are remarkably similar, considering the vast differences in time and circumstances in which each author wrote. The similarities in events, sequence, characters, and vocabulary point to the antiquity of the traditions and the deep respect of each writer for the historical remembrances of the original disciples. Yet, there are also significant differences in each of the four passion narratives as each writer provides us with a profoundly different contribution to our understanding of Jesus and the final acts of his life.

More than any other gospel, Matthew's account demonstrates that history comes to its climax in the life, death, and resurrection of Jesus. The death of Jesus is the demarcation between the old era of salvation history and the new and final age of grace. Matthew highlights this climactic reality by indicating that the final events of Jesus' life took place in fulfillment of the Old Testament scriptures. In this way he shows that the cross of Jesus was no mere unfortunate coincidence of circumstances, but was the working out of God's saving purposes for which people had waited and longed for generations.

As in Mark's gospel, the darkness over the land indicates that the day of the Lord has arrived. The final agonizing cry of Jesus, quoted in Mark's gospel in Aramaic ("Eloi, Eloi"), is quoted by Matthew in Hebrew, "Eli, Eli," which means, "my God, my God." The confusion of the crowd, thinking that Jesus was calling on Elijah, is more understandable, since "Eli" is the word from which Elijah is derived. Elijah is Israel's prophet of the end times and, in Jewish tradition, a kind of "patron saint" of hopeless cases. The rending of the temple curtain demonstrates that the new age of forgiveness has begun and that access to God's presence was now available for all.

The crucifixion of Jesus ends in Matthew's gospel not with the gloom of forsaken darkness but with dramatic signs that can be described as "apocalyptic." These signs are clear indications to those familiar with the apocalyptic writing of the Scriptures that the future has arrived. The additional signs unique to Matthew's gospel, the earthquake, the opening of tombs, the resurrection and appearance of the saints, are all the type of events prophesied for the end of the age. The quaking of the earth, as in Old Testament writings, signals God's presence and power. In Jewish literature it indicates the shaking of the old world and the breaking in of God's kingdom. The splitting of the rocks and the liberation of the holy ones from their rock tombs alludes to

Ezekiel's apocalyptic prophecy: "You shall know that I am the Lord, when I open your graves, and bring you up from your graves" (Ezek 37:13). Although the crucifixion of Jesus brings forth a new people, God does not forsake the saints of Israel.

The climactic confession of faith in Jesus, "Truly this man was God's Son!" is not made by a solitary centurion in this gospel, but by all those who were keeping watch at the cross (verse 54). The soliloquy of Mark's gospel now becomes a chorus. The community of faith formed at the cross is indeed a new people for a new era.

Reflection and discussion

• Why is the crucifixion narrative different from one gospel to the next? Why did the early church preserve all four accounts instead of only one?

• Why does Matthew allude so often to the Old Testament in his gospel account?

• How do the apocalyptic signs surrounding the death of Jesus on the cross express the meaning of that event?

Prayer

Lord of the new age, your death shook the foundations of the old order and signaled the breaking in of God's kingdom. Gather me with your disciples at the foot of the cross and enliven my hope of resurrection.

"Father, forgive them; for they do not know what they are doing." Luke 23:34

The Compassionate Savior

LUKE 23:33-49 ³³*When they came to the place that is called The Skull, they crucified Jesus there with the criminals, one on his right and one on his left.* ³⁴*Then Jesus said, "Father, forgive them; for they do not know what they are doing." And they cast lots to divide his clothing.* ³⁵*And the people stood by, watching; but the leaders scoffed at him, saying, "He saved others; let him save himself if he is the Messiah of God, his chosen one!"* ³⁶*The soldiers also mocked him, coming up and offering him sour wine,* ³⁷*and saying, "If you are the King of the Jews, save yourself!"* ³⁸*There was also an inscription over him, "This is the King of the Jews."*

³⁹*One of the criminals who were hanged there kept deriding him and saying, "Are you not the Messiah? Save yourself and us!"* ⁴⁰*But the other rebuked him, saying, "Do you not fear God, since you are under the same sentence of condemnation?* ⁴¹*And we indeed have been condemned justly, for we are getting what we deserve for our deeds, but this man has done nothing wrong."* ⁴²*Then he said, "Jesus, remember me when you come into your kingdom."* ⁴³*He replied, "Truly I tell you, today you will be with me in Paradise."*

⁴⁴*It was now about noon, and darkness came over the whole land until three in the afternoon,* ⁴⁵*while the sun's light failed; and the curtain of the temple was torn in two.* ⁴⁶*Then Jesus, crying with a loud voice, said, "Father, into your hands I commend my spirit." Having said this, he breathed his last.* ⁴⁷*When the centu-*

rion saw what had taken place, he praised God and said, "Certainly this man was innocent." [48]*And when all the crowds who had gathered there for this spectacle saw what had taken place, they returned home, beating their breasts.* [49]*But all his acquaintances, including the women who had followed him from Galilee, stood at a distance, watching these things.*

Luke's account of the crucifixion emphasizes the compassionate forgiveness Jesus offered to his persecutors and to the criminal who was crucified with him. As Jesus hung on the cross, he prayed, "Father, forgive them; for they do not know what they are doing" (verse 34). Jesus, who had urged his followers to love their enemies, now demonstrates this courageous virtue in his most extreme moment. That forgiveness is not limited to his executioners, but must surely extend to all those involved in his passion, Jews and Romans, leaders and crowds, then and now alike.

Those who watched the execution of Jesus mocked his ability to save people. The rulers said, "He saved others, let him save himself" (verse 35). The soldiers jeered, "Save yourself" (verse 37). The unrepentant criminal said, "Save yourself and us" (verse 39). The irony of their mocking is that the whole life of Jesus had been spent saving people, and his final moment on the cross would be the ultimate act of salvation in all its fullness for the world.

The two criminals crucified on each side of Jesus demonstrate quite different responses to him. One criminal continues the taunts of the crowd; the other acknowledges his wrong and puts his trust in Jesus: "Remember me when you come into your kingdom" (verses 40-42). This repentant criminal is the first person to experience the full extent of salvation Jesus offers through his death on the cross. Jesus looked at him with compassion and said, "Today you will be with me in Paradise" (verse 43). Jesus had spent his life among the outcasts; now his final act of mercy is the forgiveness of the criminal.

Trust, repentance, and forgiveness—this is the way through which the criminal on the cross came to experience the saving mercy of Jesus. Because he was with Jesus at his cross, he would be with Jesus in eternity. This process of trust, repentance, and forgiveness is the same way through which every person can come to receive Jesus' compassionate kindness. When we look to his cross, we are moved to repentance and we hear his merciful words as he reaches out to save us. The sight of Jesus with us in our pain is the promise of our healing; the sight of Jesus sharing our death is the promise of our life.

Reflection and discussion

• What is the particular emphasis of Luke's crucifixion narrative?

• What does Jesus' forgiveness of his persecutors teach me about my being called to show mercy to others?

• In what way does the experience of the criminal become my own as I look to the cross of Jesus?

Prayer

Compassionate Savior, remember me as I look upon your cross. As I receive the forgiveness that you so generously offer to me, help me to forgive anyone who needs my forgiveness today.

SUGGESTIONS FOR FACILITATORS, GROUP SESSION 2

1. If there are newcomers who were not present for the first group session, introduce them now.

2. You may want to pray this prayer as a group:

Crucified Lord, the passion accounts of Matthew, Mark, and Luke teach us the meaning of your final act of love on the cross. We read of acts of hatred and cowardice contrasted with acts of courage and faith. We look to your cross and you gather us as your freed and forgiven people. May this gathering of disciples around the cross encourage us to listen to your word, allow it to penetrate our hearts, and put it into practice in our daily lives. Bless us with your Holy Spirit as we learn together the way of discipleship.

3. Ask one or more of the following questions:
   • What was your biggest challenge in Bible study over this past week?
   • What did you learn about yourself as a disciple this week?

4. Discuss lessons 1 through 6 together. Assuming that group members have read the Scripture and commentary during the week, there is no need to read it aloud. As you review each lesson, you might want to briefly summarize the Scripture passage of each lesson and ask the group what stands out most clearly about the commentary.

5. Choose one or more of the questions for reflection and discussion from each lesson to talk over as a group. You may want to ask group members which question was most challenging or helpful to them as you review each lesson.

6. Keep the discussion moving, but don't rush the discussion in order to complete more questions. Allow time for the questions that provoke the most discussion.

7. Remember that there are no definitive answers for these discussion questions. The insights of group members will add to the understanding of all. None of these questions requires an expert.

8. Instruct group members to complete lessons 7 through 12 on their own during the six days before the next group meeting. They should write out their own answers to the questions as preparation for next week's session.

9. Conclude by praying aloud together the prayer at the end of lesson 6, or any other prayer you choose.

"Destroy this temple, and in three days I will raise it up." John 2:19

The Ruined Temple of Christ's Body

JOHN 2:13-22 ¹³*The Passover of the Jews was near, and Jesus went up to Jerusalem.* ¹⁴*In the temple he found people selling cattle, sheep, and doves, and the money changers seated at their tables.* ¹⁵*Making a whip of cords, he drove all of them out of the temple, both the sheep and the cattle. He also poured out the coins of the money changers and overturned their tables.* ¹⁶*He told those who were selling the doves, "Take these things out of here! Stop making my Father's house a market-place!"* ¹⁷*His disciples remembered that it was written, "Zeal for your house will consume me."* ¹⁸*The Jews then said to him, "What sign can you show us for doing this?"* ¹⁹*Jesus answered them, "Destroy this temple, and in three days I will raise it up."* ²⁰*The Jews then said, "This temple has been under construction for forty-six years, and will you raise it up in three days?"* ²¹*But he was speaking of the temple of his body.* ²²*After he was raised from the dead, his disciples remembered that he had said this; and they believed the scripture and the word that Jesus had spoken.*

The account of the cleansing of the temple is present in all four gospels, and in each gospel it takes place at the feast of Passover and is related to the passion and death of Jesus. Passover was the annual pilgrimage festival in Jerusalem which expressed Jewish hope for redemption and a new liberation. It was at the time of this feast that Jesus went up to Jerusalem "to depart from this world and go to the Father" (13:1) by being lifted up on the cross.

Jesus describes the temple as "my Father's house" (verse 16). The Temple was not just a place of worship, but it was honored as the place on earth where the God of Israel, the Father of Jesus, dwelt. But the gospel episode is not really about the temple itself; it is about who Jesus is. He is the one who will replace the temple in Jerusalem as the place of God's presence in the world. As the crowd challenges the actions of Jesus in the temple, he proclaims, "Destroy this temple and in three days I will raise it up" (verse 19). The crowd applied the words of Jesus literally to the temple of stone which stood before them, an edifice that had been under construction for forty-six years (verse 20). But the narrator offers us a correct understanding when he says that Jesus "was speaking about the temple of his body" (verse 21). The destruction of this body-temple is the passion and death of Jesus; the raising up in three days is his resurrection.

In John's gospel the cleansing of the temple is not an attempt by Jesus to purge the temple of commercialism, but rather an expression of his zeal for manifesting God's presence in the world. After the resurrection of Jesus the disciples are able to remember and believe both "the scripture" and "the word" Jesus spoke about the temple (verse 22). The scripture was Psalm 69:9, "Zeal for your house will consume me" (verse 17), and the word Jesus spoke was "Destroy this temple and in three days I will raise it up" (verse 19). The death and resurrection of Jesus enabled his disciples to comprehend the meaning and significance of his words and actions. Jesus was indeed "consumed," even to the point of conflict and death, by his zeal for God's house, for the presence of God in the world. But the divine presence did not require the physical temple of Jerusalem, for the Word had become flesh in the world. The temple that would be destroyed and rebuilt in three days was Jesus himself, crucified and risen, the new means of access to the unseen God, the new dwelling place of God's presence in the world.

Reflection and discussion

• What is the relationship between the destruction of the temple in Jerusalem and the destruction of Christ's body on the cross? How is Jesus the new temple of God's dwelling?

• What type of zeal consumes my life?

• What needs to be expelled from the temple of my life so that I can better experience the presence of God?

Prayer

Lord Jesus, you are the new temple not made with human hands. Accept the sacrifice of my life and unite it with your death and resurrection to become a perfect offering to the Father.

"Just as Moses lifted up the serpent in the wilderness, so must the Son of Man be lifted up." John 3:14

Lifted Sign
of Eternal Healing

JOHN 3:12-21 [12]*If I have told you about earthly things and you do not believe, how can you believe if I tell you about heavenly things?* [13]*No one has ascended into heaven except the one who descended from heaven, the Son of Man.* [14]*And just as Moses lifted up the serpent in the wilderness, so must the Son of Man be lifted up,* [15]*that whoever believes in him may have eternal life.*

[16]*"For God so loved the world that he gave his only Son, so that everyone who believes in him may not perish but may have eternal life.*

[17]*"Indeed, God did not send the Son into the world to condemn the world, but in order that the world might be saved through him.* [18]*Those who believe in him are not condemned; but those who do not believe are condemned already, because they have not believed in the name of the only Son of God.* [19]*And this is the judgment, that the light has come into the world, and people loved darkness rather than light because their deeds were evil.* [20]*For all who do evil hate the light and do not come to the light, so that their deeds may not be exposed.* [21]*But those who do what is true come to the light, so that it may be clearly seen that their deeds have been done in God."*

Jesus reveals "heavenly things" to his disciples (verse 12) because he is "the one who descended from heaven" (verse 13). He is God's unique revealer whose revelation will be most fully accomplished as he is lifted up on the cross. John states this core of his gospel by employing a Greek word with a double meaning: "lifted up" means both a physical lifting up and an exaltation. Jesus will die by being lifted up on the cross, but his crucifixion will also be his exaltation.

When the people of Israel were dying from the bites of poisonous snakes in the desert because of their sins, Moses was told by God to create a bronze serpent and raise it on a stake. All who gazed upon the uplifted serpent were restored to health (Num 21:8-9). Likewise, the Son of Man will be lifted up on the cross. All who gaze upon the elevated Jesus and believe in him, will be restored to spiritual health and receive eternal life (verses 14-15). The bronze serpent raised high in the desert becomes a gruesome intimation of Jesus nailed on the cross.

The serpent is a fearful and deadly creature; a serpent mounted on a stake is a grotesque sight. Yet the raised serpent brought restored health to God's people. The book of Wisdom describes this episode in the desert: the people were dying from the venom of the serpents and were terrorized for a while. Yet, the bronze serpent lifted on the stake became a "symbol of deliverance," and "the one who turned toward it was saved" (Wis 16:5-7). Likewise, the cross of Jesus is a fearful instrument of death; yet those who look upon it and believe, will be eternally healed.

Throughout the gospel John shows us how the wonderful gifts of God to Israel are brought to perfection in the gift of his Son to the world. The foreshadowed gifts for the small nation of Israel are completed and made universal as God sends his Son into the world (verse 17). God's intent is to save, to give eternal life, and the scope of his salvation is worldwide. This eternal life is not simply endless life; nor is it a life that begins after death. It is a new kind of life, a new order of existence that characterizes a person who is "born from above" (3:3, 7). Our most earnest wish is also God's deepest desire for us.

God's plan to bring salvation and eternal life through the "lifting up" of his Son became possible because "God so loved the world" (verse 16). If we truly understood this love of God, we would not fear anything that could possibly happen to us. In order to accept God's gift, we must "believe" in Jesus and embrace the message that he gives us. Believing in Jesus means committing ourselves to the same unselfish love that we see in Jesus, a love that found its most perfect expression in his dying on the cross for us.

Reflection and discussion

• In what way is the uplifted bronze serpent a foreshadowing of the cross of Jesus?

• What ugly or dangerous experience has become a source of growth or healing for me?

• What are the implications for me of "believing in Jesus"?

Prayer

Exalted Lord, you were lifted up on the cross so that whoever believes in you will not perish but have eternal life. As I gaze upon your uplifted cross, deepen my belief that you have the power to heal me eternally.

"Unless a grain of wheat falls into the earth and dies, it remains just a single grain; but if it dies, it bears much fruit." John 12:24

Dying Grain and Living Fruit

JOHN 12:23-33 [23]*Jesus answered them, "The hour has come for the Son of Man to be glorified.* [24]*Very truly, I tell you, unless a grain of wheat falls into the earth and dies, it remains just a single grain; but if it dies, it bears much fruit.* [25]*Those who love their life lose it, and those who hate their life in this world will keep it for eternal life.* [26]*Whoever serves me must follow me, and where I am, there will my servant be also. Whoever serves me, the Father will honor.*

[27]*"Now my soul is troubled. And what should I say—'Father, save me from this hour'? No, it is for this reason that I have come to this hour.* [28]*Father, glorify your name." Then a voice came from heaven, "I have glorified it, and I will glorify it again."* [29]*The crowd standing there heard it and said that it was thunder. Others said, "An angel has spoken to him."* [30]*Jesus answered, "This voice has come for your sake, not for mine.* [31]*Now is the judgment of this world; now the ruler of this world will be driven out.* [32]*And I, when I am lifted up from the earth, will draw all people to myself."* [33]*He said this to indicate the kind of death he was to die.*

The hour of Jesus (verses 23, 27), the dying grain of wheat (verse 24), the judgment of the world (verse 31), the lifting up from the earth, and the drawing of all people to Jesus (verse 32)—all of these are interpretations of the crucifixion of Jesus. John's gospel does not focus primarily on the historical events that led to the death of Jesus, but on the significance of that death on the cross.

Jesus proclaims that the "hour" has come. This hour is not an indication of chronological time, but implies the "significant moment of salvation." This hour in which he will be glorified (verse 23) is also the moment of his suffering. Jesus is troubled by the prospect of suffering, and he is momentarily tempted to ask the Father to save him from his passion. Yet, Jesus knows the very purpose of his life has been determined by the moment that is now upon him. This hour of Jesus' anguish and glorification is also the time of the "judgment of this world." John's gospel does not record Jesus curing those possessed by demons, as in the other gospels. Instead the saving moment of Jesus is described as one great exorcism in which "the ruler of this world will be driven out" (verse 31). The great Adversary is defeated and his captives are set free.

The image of the grain of wheat further describes the meaning of Jesus' death. Like the seed that must fall into the earth and die before it can be raised up to bear fruit, Jesus offers his own life in loving self-surrender (verse 24). Following the pattern of the germinating grain, Jesus must undergo his passion in order to be the glorious savior of all people. All who wish to follow him to eternal life must embrace this understanding of glorification in their own lives (verse 25), laying down their lives and letting go of the passing attractions of this world.

Jesus will die by being "lifted up" on the cross. But the crucifixion of Jesus will also be his exaltation: "When I am lifted up from the earth, I will draw all people to myself" (verse 32). The self-sacrifice of Jesus will draw all people to himself because nothing is more compelling or attractive than an expression of love, and no love is expressed more perfectly than that of Jesus. The cross is the power that defeats this world's powers of sin and death and draws all people like a magnet to Jesus and to his Father.

Reflection and discussion

• Why is the pattern of the germinating grain a good model for understanding Jesus?

• In what ways does the grain of wheat challenge the accepted standards of my life?

• Why does the cross of Jesus draw so many to him?

Prayer

Jesus, help me to surrender to you and let go of the passing attractions of this world. Help me to give myself to others so that my life will bear fruit for your glory.

It was the day of Preparation for the Passover; and it was about noon. Pilate said to the Jews, "Here is your King!" John 19:14

The King Mocked and Condemned

JOHN 19:1-16 *¹Then Pilate took Jesus and had him flogged. ²And the soldiers wove a crown of thorns and put it on his head, and they dressed him in a purple robe. ³They kept coming up to him, saying, "Hail, King of the Jews!" and striking him on the face. ⁴Pilate went out again and said to them, "Look, I am bringing him out to you to let you know that I find no case against him." ⁵So Jesus came out, wearing the crown of thorns and the purple robe. Pilate said to them, "Here is the man!" ⁶When the chief priests and the police saw him, they shouted, "Crucify him! Crucify him!" Pilate said to them, "Take him yourselves and crucify him; I find no case against him." ⁷The Jews answered him, "We have a law, and according to that law he ought to die because he has claimed to be the Son of God."*

⁸Now when Pilate heard this, he was more afraid than ever. ⁹He entered his headquarters again and asked Jesus, "Where are you from?" But Jesus gave him no answer. ¹⁰Pilate therefore said to him, "Do you refuse to speak to me? Do you not know that I have power to release you, and power to crucify you?" ¹¹Jesus answered him, "You would have no power over me unless it had been given you from above; therefore the one who handed me over to you is guilty of a greater sin." [12] *From then on Pilate tried to release him, but the Jews cried out, "If you release this man, you are no friend of the emperor. Everyone who claims to be a king sets himself against the emperor."*

[13] *When Pilate heard these words, he brought Jesus outside and sat on the judge's bench at a place called The Stone Pavement, or in Hebrew Gabbatha.* [14] *Now it was the day of Preparation for the Passover; and it was about noon. He said to the Jews, "Here is your King!"* [15] *They cried out, "Away with him! Away with him! Crucify him!" Pilate asked them, "Shall I crucify your King?" The chief priests answered, "We have no king but the emperor."* [16] *Then he handed him over to them to be crucified.*

Before his crucifixion, the symbols of royal power are mockingly conferred on Jesus: a purple robe and a crown of thorns. He is ridiculed by the Roman soldiers and hailed as king. Instead of acts of homage, they deliver lashes with a whip. The great irony of the scene is, of course, that Jesus is truly the king and that through him the divine source of all power is revealed. When Pilate tells Jesus that he has the power to release or crucify him, Jesus responds that whatever power he might have has been given to him by God (verses 10-11). The crucifixion in John's gospel will be expressed as an enthronement of Jesus as king, a lifting up, a moment of royal glory.

Pilate mockingly brought Jesus out for the acclamation of his people. With Jesus insultingly dressed as a king and battered by abuse, Pilate sarcastically proclaimed, "Here is the man!" (verse 5). He is presenting Jesus as a pitiful and broken man who should not be taken seriously. Yet, we know that Jesus is the suffering Son of Man on his way to glory. Vulnerable and suffering, the true kingship of Jesus was never more clearly displayed. Through this starkly memorable scene, it becomes clear that the most powerful people in the world are not the power brokers of politics and industry, but the humble, often obscure people who are true disciples of Jesus and make his presence known in the world.

Neither the Roman political authority nor the Jewish religious authority are able to recognize the truth that stands before them. Because they cannot recognize royal power in the pathetic figure of Jesus, they seek to destroy what they cannot understand. Pilate proclaims his own power, the power to release Jesus or to crucify him (verse 10); the chief priests and temple police shout,

"Crucify him!" (verse 6). Those who rely on the political or religious power of strength and intimidation believe to the end that such power solves problems. They weigh human life on the scales of convenience. Jesus shows that genuine power comes from God (verse 11) and is to be used to serve people. His power was exercised in love, a love expressed in giving his life for others. As Jesus had said, "I have power to lay it down and power to take it up again" (10:18).

The day and the time when Jesus is judged and condemned is quite significant for John's understanding of the crucifixion: "It was preparation day for Passover, and it was about noon" (verse 14). At this hour the priests of the temple began the slaughter of the lambs to be used in the Passover meal later that evening. Jesus was handed over to be crucified at the exact moment the Passover lambs were being slaughtered. Jesus is the true Lamb of God (John 1:29), preparing to be our Passover sacrifice. The offering of the great Passover Lamb would effect a liberation that would eclipse the exodus from Egypt once and for all, and would bring about a universal deliverance.

Reflection and discussion

• Who are the most powerful people I know? What is the source of their power? What power have I been given from God?

• Why is true power revealed in humility? When have I been truly strong at a time when I felt weak?

• What is significant about the day and the hour of Jesus' condemnation in John's gospel? How does this demonstrate that Jesus is the true Lamb of God?

• What is the reason for Pilate's fear (verse 8)? When have I made a decision based on fear?

• If I were Pilate, how would I explain to my wife why I had finally handed Jesus over to be crucified?

Prayer

Lamb of God, you suffered humiliation and torment so that the true power of your divinity could be revealed through your suffering humanity. Teach me humility and steadfastness so that your life may shine through my own.

Pilate also had an inscription written and put on the cross. It read, "Jesus of Nazareth, the King of the Jews." John 19:19

The Crucified King Delivered Up His Spirit

JOHN 19:17-30 *So they took Jesus;* [17] *and carrying the cross by himself, he went out to what is called The Place of the Skull, which in Hebrew is called Golgotha.* [18] *There they crucified him, and with him two others, one on either side, with Jesus between them.* [19] *Pilate also had an inscription written and put on the cross. It read, "Jesus of Nazareth, the King of the Jews."* [20] *Many of the Jews read this inscription, because the place where Jesus was crucified was near the city; and it was written in Hebrew, in Latin, and in Greek.* [21] *Then the chief priests of the Jews said to Pilate, "Do not write, 'The King of the Jews', but, 'This man said, I am King of the Jews.'"* [22] *Pilate answered, "What I have written I have written."* [23] *When the soldiers had crucified Jesus, they took his clothes and divided them into four parts, one for each soldier. They also took his tunic; now the tunic was seamless, woven in one piece from the top.* [24] *So they said to one another, "Let us not tear it, but cast lots for it to see who will get it." This was to fulfill what the scripture says,*

"They divided my clothes among themselves,
and for my clothing they cast lots."
[25] *And that is what the soldiers did.*

41

Meanwhile, standing near the cross of Jesus were his mother, and his mother's sister, Mary the wife of Clopas, and Mary Magdalene. [26] When Jesus saw his mother and the disciple whom he loved standing beside her, he said to his mother, "Woman, here is your son." [27] Then he said to the disciple, "Here is your mother." And from that hour the disciple took her into his own home.

[28] After this, when Jesus knew that all was now finished, he said (in order to fulfill the scripture), "I am thirsty." [29] A jar full of sour wine was standing there. So they put a sponge full of the wine on a branch of hyssop and held it to his mouth. [30] When Jesus had received the wine, he said, "It is finished." Then he bowed his head and gave up his spirit.

In the context of John's gospel, in which Jesus is proclaimed as the meek and majestic king who demonstrates genuine power, the crucifixion is portrayed as the most regal act in human history. The lifting up of Jesus on the cross is truly an enthronement. Above the cross is the heraldic proclamation: "Jesus of Nazareth, the King of the Jews" (verse 19). The inscription denotes a universal declaration: written in Hebrew, the language of religion; in Latin, the language of the empire; and in Greek, the language of the culture (verse 20).

At the cross the community of Jesus' disciples becomes the church. Jesus gives birth to his church by handing over his Spirit to his disciples at his death (verse 30). In preparation for and to explain the significance of this event, John describes two episodes at the foot of the cross that are unique to his gospel. In the first, John places great emphasis on the "seamless" inner garment of Jesus which is not torn apart by the Roman executioners (verses 23-24). Since the heart of Jesus' prayer for his disciples before his death was their unity (17:11, 21-22), the garment "woven in one piece" symbolized the unity of Christ's church which must not be torn apart. The outer garments are divided into four parts, representing the four corners of the world, the church's future expanse. Outer expansion and inner unity is Christ's desire for the faithful community formed at the foot of the cross.

The second episode that explains the significance of the church given birth at the cross involves the mother of Jesus and the disciple whom Jesus loved. Though Mary and the beloved disciple were historical figures, they are elevated in the gospel to symbolic figures (verses 26-27). At the cross, the mother of Jesus represents the church, the community that will give spiritual birth to future generations. The beloved disciple represents all disciples who are called to care for the church from which they receive spiritual nourishment. The beloved disciple becomes her son and the mother of Jesus becomes the mother of his disciple. The suffering of Jesus is the birth pangs of the church, because from his passion are born future generations of Christian believers (16:21). In the final act of his life, Jesus forms a new family at the cross, a family born not of blood but of faith.

On the cross Jesus had to let go, first of his possessions, specifically his clothing, then of his family, specifically his mother, and finally of life itself. John comments that "Jesus knew that all was now finished" (verse 28), indicating that Jesus knew that his mission on earth was complete. The thirst of Jesus was for final union with his Father, as proclaimed at the beginning of Psalm 63: "O God, you are my God, I seek you, my soul thirsts for you." And so Jesus uttered his final words: "It is finished" (verse 30). As he died, the text tells us that Jesus "gave up his spirit." The Greek words literally mean, "he handed over the spirit," indicating that there is more here than simply a euphemism for death. Jesus poured out the Spirit upon the infant church gathered beneath the cross. As he let go of his own life, he breathed life into the newborn community of faith

Reflection and discussion

• In what ways does the gospel indicate that the death of Jesus is the birth of his church?

• Why is the unity of his church so important to Jesus? What creates the essential unity of his disciples amidst the church's worldwide diversity?

• John's gospel notes that the mother of Jesus stood near the cross of Jesus. What might she be feeling at the end of his life?

• How do the mother of Jesus and the beloved disciple represent the new family of Jesus?

• What does the proclamation above the cross of Jesus express? Why does John's gospel note that it is in three languages?

Prayer

Crucified Lord, in your dying you have poured out your Spirit on the world. Give me grace and nourishment through your church as I seek to be your beloved disciple.

One of the soldiers pierced his side with a spear, and at once blood and water came out. John 19:34

Flowing Life from the Pierced Side of the King

JOHN 19:31-37 ³¹*Since it was the day of Preparation, the Jews did not want the bodies left on the cross during the sabbath, especially because that sabbath was a day of great solemnity. So they asked Pilate to have the legs of the crucified men broken and the bodies removed.* ³²*Then the soldiers came and broke the legs of the first and of the other who had been crucified with him.* ³³*But when they came to Jesus and saw that he was already dead, they did not break his legs.* ³⁴*Instead, one of the soldiers pierced his side with a spear, and at once blood and water came out.* ³⁵*(He who saw this has testified so that you also may believe. His testimony is true, and he knows that he tells the truth.)* ³⁶*These things occurred so that the scripture might be fulfilled, "None of his bones shall be broken."* ³⁷*And again another passage of scripture says, "They will look on the one whom they have pierced."*

Each of the gospel writers expresses the meaning of Jesus' death through signs that accompany his death. Here the unbroken bones of Jesus and the blood and water that flow from his side express truths about his death that are important for understanding its significance. John emphasizes that an eyewitness has testified to the truth of these realities and that they are preserved in the gospel "so that you may believe" (verse 35).

First, John carefully notes that the legs of the criminals were broken, while the legs of Jesus were not. The purpose of fracturing the legs was to hasten the death of the crucified victims, so that the bodies could be removed from the cross before the Sabbath began at sundown. With legs broken it was impossible for the victims to pull themselves up on the cross to breathe. But since Jesus was already dead, they did not break his legs. John's interest here is not only practical, but he clearly wants to relate Jesus' crucifixion to the feast of Passover. The passage quoted is from Exodus 12:46 which commands that none of the bones of the Passover lamb were to be broken (verse 36). Jesus is that sacrificed lamb who fulfills the ancient Passover and brings salvation to all who believe in him.

Second, John calls attention to the side of Jesus from which blood and water flow when he is pierced with a spear (verse 34). Whether this eyewitnessed phenomenon was natural or miraculous, clearly John's concern was over the meaning of this event for our understanding of Christ's death. Throughout the Scriptures, both water and blood represent life. Blood is the sacred principle of life and blood poured out sacrificially sealed covenants and atoned for sins. Water is life's most basic necessity and living water represents new life in God's Spirit. The pierced side of Jesus declares that the reality of the cross does not end in death, but in a flow of life that comes from death. That stream of life includes the sacramental life of Christ's church, the water of baptism (3:5; 7:38) and the blood of Eucharist (6:53-56). Those who look upon "the one whom they have pierced" (verse 37) are all those through the ages who recognize the significance of Christ's death on the cross.

"The Lamb of God who takes away the sin of the world" (1:29) is the title by which Jesus is introduced at the beginning of John's gospel. At the cross, the full significance of this title can be understood. Jesus is the Passover Lamb who was crucified on the day the lambs were slaughtered in the temple of Jerusalem. He is the new paschal sacrifice which brings liberation and atonement to all who put their trust in him.

Reflection and discussion

• In what ways is the death of Jesus on the cross the new and eternal Passover?

• What does the title "Lamb of God" tell me about who Jesus is for me?

• How do I experience the connections between baptism, Eucharist, and the cross of Jesus?

• In what ways has Jesus set me free from bondage? Do I live as a slave or as a free person?

Prayer

Lamb of God, who takes away the sins of the world, have mercy on me. You are my atonement sacrifice to set me free from the effects of sin and death. Help me to live confidently and victoriously in you.

SUGGESTIONS FOR FACILITATORS, GROUP SESSION 3

1. Welcome group members and ask if there are any announcements anyone would like to make.

2. You may want to pray this prayer as a group:

Lord Jesus, you are the ruined and rebuilt temple, the sign of healing lifted up, the germinating grain of wheat, the mocked, condemned, and crucified king, the Lamb of God who takes away the sin of the world. You are lifted up on the cross and we gather beneath as your disciples. Let the waters of your Spirit flow over us and sprinkle us with the blood of your sacrifice. Call us anew to follow the way of your cross and help us encourage one another.

3. Ask one or more of the following questions:
   • What new insight into the meaning of Christ's cross did you gain this week?
   • What encouragement do you need to continue on the path of Bible reading?

4. Discuss lessons 7 through 12. Choose one or more of the questions for reflection and discussion from each lesson to talk over as a group. You may want to ask group members which question was most challenging or helpful to them as you review each lesson.

5. Keep the discussion moving, but don't rush it in order to complete more questions. Allow time for the questions that provoke the most discussion.

6. After talking about each lesson, instruct group members to complete lessons 13 through 18 on their own during the six days before the next group meeting. They should write out their own answers to the questions as preparation for next week's discussion.

7. Ask the group if anyone is having any particular problems with his or her Bible study during the week. You may want to share advice and encouragement within the group.

8. Conclude by praying aloud together the prayer at the end of one of the lessons discussed. You may add to the prayer based on the sharing that has occurred in the group.

Abraham took the wood of the burnt-offering and laid it on his son Isaac, and he himself carried the fire and the knife. Gen 22:6

Sacrifice Your Only Beloved Son

GENESIS 22:1-18 ¹*After these things God tested Abraham. He said to him, "Abraham!" And he said, "Here I am." ²He said, "Take your son, your only son Isaac, whom you love, and go to the land of Moriah, and offer him there as a burnt offering on one of the mountains that I shall show you."*

³*So Abraham rose early in the morning, saddled his donkey, and took two of his young men with him, and his son Isaac; he cut the wood for the burnt offering, and set out and went to the place in the distance that God had shown him.* ⁴*On the third day Abraham looked up and saw the place far away.* ⁵*Then Abraham said to his young men, "Stay here with the donkey; the boy and I will go over there; we will worship, and then we will come back to you."* ⁶*Abraham took the wood of the burnt offering and laid it on his son Isaac, and he himself carried the fire and the knife. So the two of them walked on together.* ⁷*Isaac said to his father Abraham, "Father!" And he said, "Here I am, my son." He said, "The fire and the wood are here, but where is the lamb for a burnt offering?"* ⁸*Abraham said, "God himself will provide the lamb for a burnt offering, my son." So the two of them walked on together.*

⁹*When they came to the place that God had shown him, Abraham built an*

49

altar there and laid the wood in order. He bound his son Isaac, and laid him on the altar, on top of the wood. [10] *Then Abraham reached out his hand and took the knife to kill his son.* [11] *But the angel of the Lord called to him from heaven, and said, "Abraham, Abraham!" And he said, "Here I am."* [12] *He said, "Do not lay your hand on the boy or do anything to him; for now I know that you fear God, since you have not withheld your son, your only son, from me."* [13] *And Abraham looked up and saw a ram, caught in a thicket by its horns. Abraham went and took the ram and offered it up as a burnt offering instead of his son.* [14] *So Abraham called that place "The Lord will provide"; as it is said to this day, "On the mount of the Lord it shall be provided."*

[15] *The angel of the Lord called to Abraham a second time from heaven,* [16] *and said, "By myself I have sworn, says the Lord: Because you have done this, and have not withheld your son, your only son,* [17] *I will indeed bless you, and I will make your offspring as numerous as the stars of heaven and as the sand that is on the seashore. And your offspring shall possess the gate of their enemies,* [18] *and by your offspring shall all the nations of the earth gain blessing for themselves, because you have obeyed my voice."*

The story of the sacrifice of Isaac describes Abraham's greatest trial and his willingness to obey God's word in all its mysterious harshness. The account presents the unfathomable will of God, whose ways are mysterious, yet whose final word is mercy and grace. It gave God's people a model of complete obedience to God in times of testing, teaching them that God would always prove to be worthy of their trust. As the early Christians sought to understand the mystery of the cross, they found hints of God's plan in this story of Israel's patriarchs.

The test required that Isaac should be killed as a sacrifice. Worse still, Abraham himself was to put his son to death. Isaac was Abraham's uniquely beloved son (verses 2, 12, 16), the child of promise for whom Abraham and Sarah had waited interminably. He was the child on whom the future fulfillment of God's promises to Abraham depended. The test was severe, yet the response was superb.

Like Isaac, Jesus was his Father's only beloved Son. At the foot of the mountain where the sacrifice was to take place, "Abraham took the wood of the burnt-offering and laid it on his son Isaac" (verse 6). The words remind

Christian readers of the way Jesus went to the hill of Golgotha, according to John, "carrying the cross by himself" (John 19:17). Isaac, like Jesus, submitted willingly as he was bound and prepared for sacrifice. In a dramatic reversal of verse 6, where the wood was laid on top of Isaac, he himself was now laid on top of the wood (verse 9). Jesus, the new sacrifice, was bound to the wood of the cross which he had carried to the place of sacrifice.

With split-second timing as Abraham was about to slay his son, God's angel called Abraham for a second time, decisively revoking the original command. Abraham had proven totally faithful and discovered that God is the Lord who provides (verse 14). Abraham's evasive reply to Isaac, "God himself will provide the lamb for a burnt-offering" (verse 8), proved prophetic. God provided the ram at the exact time Abraham needed it (verse 13), but God would provide for his people supremely in Christ. The Lamb God provides, the Lamb who is his Son, offers himself in sacrifice and takes away the sin of the world. God provided a substitute sacrifice so that Abraham and his son could go free and return home together with a renewed promise of blessings (verses 16-18). The substitute sacrifice of the Lamb of God on Calvary gains our eternal freedom and offers us the promise of abundant life.

Tradition identifies Moriah, "the mount of the Lord" (verses 2, 14), as the temple mount in Jerusalem (2 Chron 3:1). Jesus became the new sacrifice and the new temple as he offered his life in Jerusalem. The threads of God's plan woven throughout salvation history lead to the cross of Jesus.

Reflection and discussion

• How is Jesus like both Isaac and the lamb that God would provide?

• What is the most difficult thing I've ever been asked to do? Where did I get the strength to do it?

• What did God really want from Abraham?

• Why did the early Christians turn to this text for insights into the meaning of Christ's cross?

• What evidence do I have that God's final word is always mercy and grace?

Prayer

God, you so loved the world that you gave your only Son for us. Thank you for redeeming me through the sacrifice of Jesus on the cross. Help me to trust in your power to save me from eternal death.

"The blood shall be a sign for you on the houses where you live: when I see the blood, I will pass over you." Exod 12:13

The Saving Blood of the Lord's Passover

EXODUS 12:1-14 *¹The Lord said to Moses and Aaron in the land of Egypt: ²This month shall mark for you the beginning of months; it shall be the first month of the year for you. ³Tell the whole congregation of Israel that on the tenth of this month they are to take a lamb for each family, a lamb for each household. ⁴If a household is too small for a whole lamb, it shall join its closest neighbor in obtaining one; the lamb shall be divided in proportion to the number of people who eat of it. ⁵Your lamb shall be without blemish, a year-old male; you may take it from the sheep or from the goats. ⁶You shall keep it until the fourteenth day of this month; then the whole assembled congregation of Israel shall slaughter it at twilight. ⁷They shall take some of the blood and put it on the two doorposts and the lintel of the houses in which they eat it. ⁸They shall eat the lamb that same night; they shall eat it roasted over the fire with unleavened bread and bitter herbs. ⁹Do not eat any of it raw or boiled in water, but roasted over the fire, with its head, legs, and inner organs. ¹⁰You shall let none of it remain until the morning; anything that remains until the morning you shall burn. ¹¹This is how you shall eat it: your loins girded, your sandals on your feet, and your staff in your hand; and you shall eat it hurriedly. It is the passover of the Lord. ¹²For I will pass* *through the land of Egypt that night, and I will strike down every firstborn in the land of Egypt, both human beings and animals; on all the gods of Egypt I will execute judgments: I am the Lord.* ¹³*The blood shall be a sign for you on the houses where you live: when I see the blood, I will pass over you, and no plague shall destroy you when I strike the land of Egypt.* ¹⁴*This day shall be a day of remembrance for you. You shall celebrate it as a festival to the Lord; throughout your generations you shall observe it as a perpetual ordinance.*

The harsh oppression of the Israelites could not help but rouse the God of justice, love, and mercy to come to their rescue. The book of Exodus uses a rich variety of verbs to describe this process: God rescues, delivers, brings out, saves, and redeems his people. The exodus was initiated and achieved by God, who acted in power, justice, compassion, and covenant-faithfulness.

The sacrifice of the Passover lamb and the sprinkling of its blood on the doorposts of the Israelite homes preserved God's chosen people from the destruction visited upon the Egyptians. God said, "Seeing the blood, I will pass over you" (verse 13). Passover became a central memorial feast for Israel, celebrated as an annual pilgrimage festival in Jerusalem at the time of Jesus and later ritualized in every Jewish home. It is a celebration of liberation, a commemoration of God's freeing the Israelites from bondage and bringing them into the freedom which allowed them to become a covenanted people.

The chosen lamb was to be "without blemish" (verse 5), meaning that the Israelites were to offer God the best of their flock, not a sick or weak animal. When the lamb was slaughtered, its blood was not only poured out but also applied to the top and the sides of the doorframe of each home (verse 7). The lamb was then roasted and eaten by the family, meaning that the lamb was not only a sacrificial substitute, shedding its life for their own, but also a source of nourishment.

The gospels associate the passion and death of Jesus with the Passover feast. At the Last Supper Jesus gave his body and blood to his disciples in the bread and wine of the Passover meal and his blood was shed on the cross on the day of the feast itself. John's gospel proclaims that Jesus is the Lamb of God (John 1:29) and indicates that his death on the cross occurred as the Passover lambs were being slaughtered at the temple (John 19:14). John notes too that none of the bones of Jesus were fractured, which he interprets as a fulfillment of the prescription about the Passover Lamb: "You shall not break any of its bones" (Exod 12:46; John 19:31-36).

The events of Passover night were the defining events of Israel's history. Passover revealed God's faithfulness to his word. It fashioned their understanding of God and their identity as God's people. In the historical understanding of Israel, the exodus to freedom would not have happened without the Passover. Too often people want liberation without the blood, salvation without the sacrifice, and forgiveness without the cross. Christ, our paschal lamb, was sacrificed to liberate, rescue, deliver, redeem, and save God's people from the sin of the world.

Reflection and discussion

• What did the flesh and blood of the lamb do for the people of Israel?

• In light of the Passover, why was it "necessary" that Christ suffer and shed his blood? What does the Passover reveal to me about the nature of God?

Prayer

Lamb of God, who takes away the sin of the world, have mercy on me. You have given your life for me and shed your blood for my redemption. Free me from all that impedes me from experiencing the fullness of life.

On this day atonement shall be made for you, to cleanse you; from all your sins you shall be clean before the Lord. Lev 16:30

The Day of Atonement

LEVITICUS 16:1-22 ¹*The Lord spoke to Moses after the death of the two sons of Aaron, when they drew near before the Lord and died.* ²*The Lord said to Moses: Tell your brother Aaron not to come just at any time into the sanctuary inside the curtain before the mercy seat that is upon the ark, or he will die; for I appear in the cloud upon the mercy seat.* ³*Thus shall Aaron come into the holy place: with a young bull for a sin offering and a ram for a burnt offering.* ⁴*He shall put on the holy linen tunic, and shall have the linen undergarments next to his body, fasten the linen sash, and wear the linen turban; these are the holy vestments. He shall bathe his body in water, and then put them on.* ⁵*He shall take from the congregation of the people of Israel two male goats for a sin offering, and one ram for a burnt offering.*

⁶*Aaron shall offer the bull as a sin offering for himself, and shall make atonement for himself and for his house.* ⁷*He shall take the two goats and set them before the Lord at the entrance of the tent of meeting;* ⁸*and Aaron shall cast lots on the two goats, one lot for the Lord and the other lot for Azazel.* ⁹*Aaron shall present the goat on which the lot fell for the Lord, and offer it as a sin offering;* ¹⁰*but the goat on which the lot fell for Azazel shall be presented alive before the Lord to make atonement over it, that it may be sent away into the wilderness to Azazel.*

¹¹*Aaron shall present the bull as a sin offering for himself, and shall make atonement for himself and for his house; he shall slaughter the bull as a sin offering for himself.* ¹²*He shall take a censer full of coals of fire from the altar before the Lord, and two handfuls of crushed sweet incense, and he shall bring it inside the curtain* ¹³*and put the incense on the fire before the Lord, that the cloud of the incense may cover the mercy seat that is upon the covenant, or he will die.* ¹⁴*He shall take some of the blood of the bull, and sprinkle it with his finger on the front of the mercy seat, and before the mercy seat he shall sprinkle the blood with his finger seven times.*

¹⁵*He shall slaughter the goat of the sin offering that is for the people and bring its blood inside the curtain, and do with its blood as he did with the blood of the bull, sprinkling it upon the mercy seat and before the mercy seat.* ¹⁶*Thus he shall make atonement for the sanctuary, because of the uncleannesses of the people of Israel, and because of their transgressions, all their sins; and so he shall do for the tent of meeting, which remains with them in the midst of their uncleannesses.* ¹⁷*No one shall be in the tent of meeting from the time he enters to make atonement in the sanctuary until he comes out and has made atonement for himself and for his house and for all the assembly of Israel.* ¹⁸*Then he shall go out to the altar that is before the Lord and make atonement on its behalf, and shall take some of the blood of the bull and of the blood of the goat, and put it on each of the horns of the altar.* ¹⁹*He shall sprinkle some of the blood on it with his finger seven times, and cleanse it and hallow it from the uncleannesses of the people of Israel.*

²⁰*When he has finished atoning for the holy place and the tent of meeting and the altar, he shall present the live goat.* ²¹*Then Aaron shall lay both his hands on the head of the live goat, and confess over it all the iniquities of the people of Israel, and all their transgressions, all their sins, putting them on the head of the goat, and sending it away into the wilderness by means of someone designated for the task.* ²²*The goat shall bear on itself all their iniquities to a barren region; and the goat shall be set free in the wilderness.*

Like Passover, the feast of Yom Kippur (the Day of Atonement) began in the exodus and continued in an annual ritual in Jerusalem. The complex rituals are described at the pivotal center of the book of Leviticus, as the climax of its laws of sacrifice, priestly service, and purity. On this supremely important day, the impurities of the sanctuary, priests, and people were removed, repairing Israel's relationship with God.

Only on this one day each year could the high priest pass beyond the curtain of the sanctuary and enter the Holy of Holies. Because entering the presence of God was such a dangerous venture, Aaron and the high priests who succeeded him were required to prepare and to follow a prescribed ritual lest they should die during the encounter (verses 1-2). On this singular day, the high priest was to lay aside the splendid, ornate garments of his office and clothe himself in a white, linen garment (verse 4) as an expression of the humility and penitential attitude necessary to perform his sacred duties.

After offering a bull for his own sin offering and a goat for that of the people, the high priest entered the Holy of Holies to officiate in the presence of God. He brought with him a censer full of fiery coals and finely ground incense. The smoke from the incense upon the coals obscured the divine presence so that God's majestic holiness would be bearable by a sinful man (verse 12). He then sprinkled the sacrificial blood, first of the bull and then of the goat, upon the "mercy-seat" which covered the Ark of the Covenant in order to atone for his own sins and for the sins of the people (verses 14-15). Since blood is the essence of life (17:11), the shedding of blood in sacrifice symbolizes a life laid down on behalf of others and the sprinkling of the blood applies the effects of the sacrifice, bringing cleansing and forgiveness.

The rituals of atonement for the sins of the people were performed with two goats. One goat was sacrificed as a sin offering to the Lord; the other was designated as the scapegoat, to be sent away to Azazel, the demon of the harsh wilderness (verses 8-10). The high priest places both hands on the live goat's head, confessing all the sins of Israel over it, and sends it away into the desert (verses 20-22). The people's sins are thus removed as far away as possible and done away with. Sin does not belong with God's covenanted people, so it is taken back to its source among the wild spirits of the wilderness.

The report of Yom Kippur describes the impurities which alienate God from his people using a variety of terms: uncleanness, transgressions, iniquities, and sins (verses 16, 21). The rites for the Day of Atonement remove impurities from all Israel, through rites of sacrifice and riddance, beginning in the most sacred place and extending to the farthest fringes. Atonement is an act of God in his own dwelling place which leads to the removal of sin as far away as possible.

Reflection and discussion

• What do the high priest's rigorous preparations for his annual entry into the Holy of Holies tell me about the Israelite understanding of God?

• What are the effects of sacrificial blood in atoning for sins?

• Why are rituals of reconciliation important? What does the annual Day of Atonement tell me about human nature?

Prayer

God of the covenant, you are awesome in power and majestic in holiness. Sin alienates me from your generous and loving presence. Cleanse and forgive me of my wrong and dwell with me all the days of my life.

He poured out himself to death, and was numbered with the transgressors;
yet he bore the sin of many, and made intercession for the transgressors.

Isa 53:12

He Bore Our Infirmities and Endured Our Sufferings

ISAIAH 53:1-12 *¹Who has believed what we have heard?*
And to whom has the arm of the Lord been revealed?
²For he grew up before him like a young plant,
*   and like a root out of dry ground;*
he had no form or majesty that we should look at him,
*   nothing in his appearance that we should desire him.*
³He was despised and rejected by others;
*   a man of suffering and acquainted with infirmity;*
and as one from whom others hide their faces
*   he was despised, and we held him of no account.*
⁴Surely he has borne our infirmities
*   and carried our diseases;*
yet we accounted him stricken,
*   struck down by God, and afflicted.*
⁵But he was wounded for our transgressions,
*   crushed for our iniquities;*

upon him was the punishment that made us whole,
   and by his bruises we are healed.
⁶All we like sheep have gone astray;
   we have all turned to our own way,
and the Lord has laid on him
   the iniquity of us all.

⁷He was oppressed, and he was afflicted,
   yet he did not open his mouth;
like a lamb that is led to the slaughter,
   and like a sheep that before its shearers is silent,
   so he did not open his mouth.
⁸By a perversion of justice he was taken away.
   Who could have imagined his future?
For he was cut off from the land of the living,
   stricken for the transgression of my people.
⁹They made his grave with the wicked
   and his tomb with the rich,
although he had done no violence,
   and there was no deceit in his mouth.

¹⁰Yet it was the will of the Lord to crush him with pain.
When you make his life an offering for sin,
   he shall see his offspring, and shall prolong his days;
through him the will of the Lord shall prosper.
   ¹¹Out of his anguish he shall see light;
he shall find satisfaction through his knowledge.
   The righteous one, my servant, shall make many righteous,
   and he shall bear their iniquities.
¹²Therefore I will allot him a portion with the great,
   and he shall divide the spoil with the strong;
because he poured out himself to death,
   and was numbered with the transgressors;
yet he bore the sin of many,
   and made intercession for the transgressors.

Several passages from the later part of Isaiah are referred to as the Suffering Servant songs (Isa 42:1–9; 49:1–7; 50:4–11; 52:13—53:12). This mysterious figure, spoken about by Isaiah over five hundred years before the coming of Jesus, is chosen by God to take on the sin and sufferings of others. The Servant seems to be a failure, suffering a shameful and unjust death. Yet through his trials, the Servant accomplishes God's saving will, bringing justification and life not only for Israel but for all the nations (49:6). No other passages from the Old Testament speak more eloquently of the mystery of the cross.

God's Servant is despised and rejected (verse 3); he is stricken, smitten, and afflicted (verse 4). Yet, the Servant is innocent and his suffering is for the sake of others: "He was wounded for our transgressions, crushed for our iniquities" (verse 5). He is a vicarious sufferer, taking upon himself the suffering that others deserved. As a result of his ordeal, others are healed and made whole (verse 5). Reading verses 5 and 6 again, we realize that whoever the "we" and "us" were in Israel's history, this passage now includes us all. We have gone astray and turned away. God "has laid upon him the iniquity of us all," like the guilt of the people was laid on the sin offerings and the scapegoat on the Day of Atonement. In him our sin finds forgiveness, our brokenness is made whole, our spiritual illness is healed.

Like the silent lamb led to the slaughter, the Servant was quiet and unprotesting as he made his way to death (verse 7). Subjected to an unjust trial, he was led from the court to his execution, cut off and stricken with a violent death (verse 8). Innocent to the end, he was buried like a common criminal (verse 9). Finally, the writer expresses the meaning of the suffering, informing us that the Servant's life was an offering for sin (verse 10), that he bore our iniquities and the sins of many (verses 11-12), and that he made intercession for transgressors (verse 12).

Throughout salvation history, God's people have struggled to understand how God would break the pattern of sin and punishment and replace it with forgiveness and compassion. The system of animal sacrifice was a partial answer to that dilemma, but it was inadequate. The work of the Suffering Servant is modeled on the ancient rites of the Day of Atonement, yet it far surpasses them because the sacrifice offered is a human person. Since sin involves the will and animals cannot willingly offer themselves, animals can never fully substitute for people. The Servant offered himself personally, consciously, and deliberately, doing what sheep, goats, and bulls could never do.

Who was this Suffering Servant? Prophecy is capable of multiple fulfillment, and this prophecy was fulfilled progressively in the prophet himself, in
various kings of Israel, and collectively in the Jewish people, before it was fulfilled definitively in Jesus on the cross. These passages from Isaiah reverber-
ate throughout the passion narratives of the four gospels, and clearly the disciples of Jesus read these prophetic verses to help them understand the suffering and death of Jesus. Because of the testimony of the Old Testament, the
early Christians realized that God chose to accomplish his saving will through
suffering, that God redeemed us through the sacrifice of Christ, and that he
forgave us and healed us forever through the cross of Jesus.

Reflection and discussion

• How does the offering of the Suffering Servant surpass the practice of animal sacrifice and bring us closer to the cross of Jesus?

• What parts of the passion narratives of the gospels echo the prophecy of the
Suffering Servant?

Prayer

*Suffering Servant of God, you have taken my sins upon yourself and have
suffered in place of me. Help me to trust in the power of your sacrifice to
heal me and free me from guilt.*

"Only know for certain that if you put me to death, you will be bringing inno-cent blood upon yourselves and upon this city and its inhabitants." Jer 26:15

The Passion Account of the Prophet

JEREMIAH 26:7-19 *⁷The priests and the prophets and all the people heard Jeremiah speaking these words in the house of the Lord. ⁸And when Jeremiah had finished speaking all that the Lord had commanded him to speak to all the people, then the priests and the prophets and all the people laid hold of him, saying, "You shall die! ⁹Why have you prophesied in the name of the Lord, saying, "This house shall be like Shiloh, and this city shall be desolate, without inhabitant'?" And all the people gathered around Jeremiah in the house of the Lord.*

¹⁰When the officials of Judah heard these things, they came up from the king's house to the house of the Lord and took their seat in the entry of the New Gate of the house of the Lord. ¹¹Then the priests and the prophets said to the offi-cials and to all the people, "This man deserves the sentence of death because he has prophesied against this city, as you have heard with your own ears."

¹²Then Jeremiah spoke to all the officials and all the people, saying, "It is the Lord who sent me to prophesy against this house and this city all the words you have heard. ¹³Now therefore amend your ways and your doings, and obey the voice of the Lord your God, and the Lord will change his mind about the disas-ter that he has pronounced against you. ¹⁴But as for me, here I am in your hands.

Do with me as seems good and right to you. ¹⁵*Only know for certain that if you put me to death, you will be bringing innocent blood upon yourselves and upon this city and its inhabitants, for in truth the Lord sent me to you to speak all these words in your ears."*

¹⁶*Then the officials and all the people said to the priests and the prophets, "This man does not deserve the sentence of death, for he has spoken to us in the name of the Lord our God."* ¹⁷*And some of the elders of the land arose and said to all the assembled people,* ¹⁸*"Micah of Moresheth, who prophesied during the days of King Hezekiah of Judah, said to all the people of Judah: 'Thus says the Lord of hosts,*

> *Zion shall be plowed as a field;*
>> *Jerusalem shall become a heap of ruins,*
>>> *and the mountain of the house a wooded height.'*

¹⁹*Did King Hezekiah of Judah and all Judah actually put him to death? Did he not fear the Lord and entreat the favor of the Lord, and did not the Lord change his mind about the disaster that he had pronounced against them? But we are about to bring great disaster on ourselves!"*

If Isaiah spoke about a Suffering Servant of God, Jeremiah lived the life of a suffering servant of God. The words and deeds of Jeremiah recounted in the book of the prophet, along with a narrative of his suffering and rejection, form what might be called a "passion account of Jeremiah." This narrative includes Jeremiah's warnings about the destruction of the temple, his confrontation with the religious authorities of Jerusalem, the plotting against him, the participation of all the people, the abandonment by his friends, Jeremiah's deep sorrow and his wish to be released from his mission, and his death sentence. As the early Christians reread this passion of Jeremiah they could grasp its fuller prophetic significance for understanding the suffering and death of Jesus.

Both Jeremiah and Jesus ministered just before the fall of Jerusalem and the destruction of the temple: Jeremiah before the first destruction in the 6th century B.C., and Jesus before the second destruction in the 1st century A.D. Like Jesus, Jeremiah preached about the pending destruction of Jerusalem and its temple: "It is the Lord who sent me to prophesy against this house and this city" (verse 12). It was this preaching that enraged the religious officials of Judah against both Jeremiah and Jesus. They both wept over Jerusalem and were unjustly accused of political treason. Their prophetic words and actions against the temple set the religious officials to plot their death. The priests and the prophets said to the princes and all the people, "This man deserves the sentence of death" (verse 11). Yet Jeremiah, like Jesus, was innocent of the charges brought by the religious officials. Jeremiah proclaimed, "If you put me to death, you will be bringing innocent blood upon yourselves and upon this city and its inhabitants" (verse 15). Both Jeremiah and Jesus were tried, persecuted, and imprisoned. Tradition holds that eventually Jeremiah was violently put to death by his own people.

Jeremiah, like Jesus, suffered for the message he proclaimed. But all his suffering never altered his message. He faithfully spoke God's truth even when it cost him his safety and security. When his life was threatened, Jeremiah said, "I was like a gentle lamb led to the slaughter" (11:19). Though Jeremiah was not crucified, he experienced the rejection, accusations, pain, and abandonment of Jesus on the cross. For many of the prophets of the Old Testament, their words found fulfillment in the life and death of Jesus. But with Jeremiah, his deeds as well as his words found fulfillment in Christ. His life was a foreshadowing or prototype of the ministry of Jesus.

Reflection and discussion

• What was similar about the time periods in which Jeremiah and Jesus ministered?

• What parts of the life of Jesus show him to be a prophet like Jeremiah?

• Which parts of Jeremiah's life foreshadow the passion and cross of Jesus?

• In what ways does the preaching of Jeremiah and Jesus about the temple enrage the religious authorities to plot their death?

• How have I suffered for speaking or living the truth? Am I willing to undergo rejection and abandonment for living in a way that contradicts the ways accepted in our society?

Prayer

Lord God, your prophets in each generation suffered for the message they proclaimed. Help me listen to your prophets today and witness to the truth of the Gospel. May the deeds of my life express the faith I believe.

All who see me mock at me; they make mouths at me,
they shake their heads. Ps 22:7

Why Have You Forsaken Me?

PSALM 22:1-21 ¹*My God, my God, why have you forsaken me?*
  Why are you so far from helping me, from the words of my groaning?
²*O my God, I cry by day, but you do not answer;*
  and by night, but find no rest.

³*Yet you are holy,*
  enthroned on the praises of Israel.
⁴*In you our ancestors trusted;*
  they trusted, and you delivered them.
⁵*To you they cried, and were saved;*
  in you they trusted, and were not put to shame.

⁶*But I am a worm, and not human;*
  scorned by others, and despised by the people.
⁷*All who see me mock at me;*
  they make mouths at me, they shake their heads;
⁸*"Commit your cause to the Lord;*
  let him deliver— let him rescue the one in whom he delights!"

⁹ Yet it was you who took me from the womb;
  you kept me safe on my mother's breast.
¹⁰ On you I was cast from my birth,
  and since my mother bore me you have been my God.
¹¹ Do not be far from me,
  for trouble is near
  and there is no one to help.

¹² Many bulls encircle me,
  strong bulls of Bashan surround me;
¹³ they open wide their mouths at me,
  like a ravening and roaring lion.

¹⁴ I am poured out like water,
  and all my bones are out of joint;
my heart is like wax;
  it is melted within my breast;
¹⁵ my mouth is dried up like a potsherd,
  and my tongue sticks to my jaws;
  you lay me in the dust of death.

¹⁶ For dogs are all around me;
  a company of evildoers encircles me.
My hands and feet have shriveled;
¹⁷ I can count all my bones.
They stare and gloat over me;
¹⁸ they divide my clothes among themselves,
  and for my clothing they cast lots.

¹⁹ But you, O Lord, do not be far away!
  O my help, come quickly to my aid!
²⁰ Deliver my soul from the sword,
  my life from the power of the dog!
  ²¹ Save me from the mouth of the lion!
From the horns of the wild oxen you have rescued me.

In the gospels of Mark and Matthew the final words of Jesus before his death are the opening verse of Psalm 22: "My God, my God, why have you forsaken me?" The gospel writers communicate the words in the original Aramaic and Hebrew languages, one of which Jesus must have spoken from the cross (Matt 27:46; Mark 15:34). The words came to Jesus' mind, perhaps instinctively, to express his experience of torment and the feeling of abandonment. The God with whom Jesus had enjoyed close intimacy and affirmation throughout his life, now seemed to have deserted him.

Jesus must have experienced on the cross what many have called a "dark night of the soul." In this experience Jesus was united with the many people who struggle with not only severe physical suffering, but emotional and spiritual affliction as well. The pain is enormous when a person knows that God is good and loving, yet experiences only betrayal and desolation. Jesus plunged into the very human experience of God's silence when most in need.

In quoting the first verse of the psalm, however, the evangelists want the reader to recall the entire psalm. Several other verses of the psalm are quoted or alluded to in the passion accounts. Surely Jesus, who knew the psalms by heart, must have continued the psalm as his final prayer to the Father. The prayer is the lament of a tortured Israelite who is suffering unjustly. The first half of the psalm (verses 1-21) focuses on the desolation of his suffering; the second half (verses 22-31) on the triumphant vindication of God's faithful one.

For Christians, Jesus is the fullest embodiment of this faithful Israelite. Abandoned by his friends and seemingly by God (verses 1-2, 6), mocked and tormented by his enemies (verses 7-8), his garments divided by lot (verse 18), his hands and feet pierced (verse 16), and thirsting for drink (verse 15), Jesus placed his life solely in God's hands. The early Christians used this psalm, as they used other parts of the Old Testament, to emphasize its fulfillment in the passion of Jesus and to interpret the full meaning of his torturous death as a surrender of his life to his Father.

The identification of Jesus' experience with that of the psalmist does not end with the lament section, however. Both experience the deliverance of God expressed in the psalm's second half; whereas the psalmist is delivered *from* death, Jesus is delivered *through* death. The forsaken one, after expressing his lament, gives praise to God who hears his cry (verse 24) and receives the praise of nations and future generations (verses 27-31).

Reflection and discussion

• In what ways is this psalm an apt and accurate portrayal of the sufferings of Jesus?

• When have I felt abandoned by God and by other people?

• Which verses speak most eloquently of my sorrow and my hope?

Prayer

My God, my God, when I am suffering alone and feeling abandoned, help me to trust in you. When I am mocked and surrounded by evil, protect me and do not turn your face from me. May I proclaim your faithfulness to the coming generation.

SUGGESTIONS FOR FACILITATORS, GROUP SESSION 4

1. Welcome group members and ask if anyone has any questions, announcements, or requests.

2. You may want to pray this prayer as a group:

Lord Jesus, the words of the ancient Hebrew Scriptures find their fullest expression in you. You are the beloved Son given by the Father, the new Passover, the sacrifice offered for the atonement of all, the Suffering Servant, the tormented prophet, and the forsaken Israelite of the psalms. As we read the Old Testament, give us a rich appreciation of the historical circumstances of the ancient writers and also enable us to see the fuller meaning that anticipates your life, death, and resurrection. Help us to trust in your power to deliver us from darkness, pain, fear, and insecurity.

3. Ask one or more of the following questions:
   - What is the most difficult part of this study for you?
   - What did you learn about the Old Testament this week?

4. Discuss lessons 13 through 18. Choose one or more of the questions for reflection and discussion from each lesson to discuss as a group. You may want to ask group members which question was most challenging or helpful to them as you review each lesson.

5. Keep the discussion moving, but allow time for the questions that provoke the most discussion. Encourage the group members to use "I" language in their responses.

6. After talking over each lesson, instruct group members to complete lessons 19 through 24 on their own during the six days before the next group meeting. They should write out their own answers to the questions as preparation for next week's session.

7. Conclude by praying aloud together the prayer at the end of one of the lessons discussed. You may choose to conclude the prayer by asking members to pray aloud any requests they may have.

We proclaim Christ crucified, a stumbling block to Jews and foolishness to Gentiles, but to those who are the called, both Jews and Greeks, Christ the power of God and the wisdom of God. 1 Cor 1:23-24

The Scandalous Message of the Cross

1 CORINTHIANS 1:18-25; 2:1-5 ¹⁸*For the message about the cross is foolishness to those who are perishing, but to us who are being saved it is the power of God.* ¹⁹*For it is written,*

> *"I will destroy the wisdom of the wise,*
>   *and the discernment of the discerning I will thwart."*

²⁰*Where is the one who is wise? Where is the scribe? Where is the debater of this age? Has not God made foolish the wisdom of the world?* ²¹*For since, in the wisdom of God, the world did not know God through wisdom, God decided, through the foolishness of our proclamation, to save those who believe.* ²²*For Jews demand signs and Greeks desire wisdom,* ²³*but we proclaim Christ crucified, a stumbling block to Jews and foolishness to Gentiles,* ²⁴*but to those who are the called, both Jews and Greeks, Christ the power of God and the wisdom of God.* ²⁵*For God's foolishness is wiser than human wisdom, and God's weakness is stronger than human strength.*

2 ¹*When I came to you, brothers and sisters, I did not come proclaiming the mystery of God to you in lofty words or wisdom.* ²*For I decided to know nothing among you except Jesus Christ, and him crucified.* ³*And I came to you in weakness and in fear and in much trembling.* ⁴*My speech and my proclamation were not with plausible words of wisdom, but with a demonstration of the Spirit and of power,* ⁵*so that your faith might rest not on human wisdom but on the power of God.*

Paul's words proclaim the paradox of the cross: "foolishness to those who are perishing," but for those being saved, "it is the power of God" (verse 18). Human wisdom has never been able to understand what God is doing in the world. In the logic of human wisdom the cross seems embarrassing and tragic. The cross represents the ultimate in human weakness; it expresses failure, oppression, utter defeat. In a world where the cross was seen as the most horrid and barbaric form of punishment imaginable, the gospel about a crucified Savior seemed to be utter madness. Both Jews and Greeks considered the cross absurd.

Yet, in the crucifixion of his Son, God has surpassed human wisdom and acted powerfully to save us from sin and death. Indeed, through the cross God has turned human wisdom on its head. The meaning of the cross has been transformed by the person who is stretched out upon it and by the God who "destroys the wisdom of the wise" (verse 19). Now the cross expresses a life given for others, service instead of exploitation, hope in the midst of suffering, and ultimate victory over the greatest evils, the powers of sin and death.

The Jews believed that if God were to visit this world with salvation, it would be in power. They were looking for a Messiah who would perform great works of liberation for them. This fed their appetite for the sensational and miraculous. They insisted upon "signs" (verse 22). There were many false messiahs during Paul's lifetime, all of them promising to perform great wonders. Jesus had consistently been asked during his life to produce a sign. But the primary sign that Jesus produced was the sign of the cross. For the Jews, the cross of Jesus was a "stumbling-block" (verse 23). It spoke of weakness, not power; of defeat, not victory; of humiliation, not conquest. A crucified Messiah sounded like a contradiction in terms. It was inconceivable that the Messiah could suffer such a disgraceful and humiliating death.

The Gentile Greeks, on the other hand, sought to know God through reasoned argument. They could not conceive of a man having wisdom yet not having sufficient wit to save himself from so ghastly a death. That God would manifest himself in human flesh and claim to save the world in such a savage and naïve way was silliness. They followed those who used silver-tongued speech and persuasive rhetoric. Looking for logic and reason, they found the message of the cross to be utter foolishness (verses 22-23).

It seemed that the Christian message had little chance of success among the Jews or the Greeks. Yet, Paul proclaimed that the cross is the power and wisdom of God (verse 24). In the cross God was outsmarting the world and replacing its prideful arrogance and illusions. In surrendering himself to weakness and folly, God establishes his true wisdom and demonstrates his mighty authority. Here was truth that could not be argued with reason or imposed with power. It had to be revealed, as the apostles proclaimed the gospel of Jesus Christ crucified, and as the Spirit gave insight that enabled people to understand the saving message of the cross.

Reflection and discussion

• Why did the message of the cross seem to be such madness to people of the first century?

• Why would God choose to manifest himself in weakness, defeat, and humiliation?

• Why was a crucified messiah so inconceivable for many Jews?

• What was the primary barrier to accepting the cross for the Gentile Greeks?

• What message am I proclaiming when I wear a cross on my neck or hang a crucifix in my home?

Prayer

Crucified and glorious Lord, help me to embrace the mystery of your cross as the center of my life. Though it seems foolish in the eyes of the world, I proclaim you as my crucified Savior and I rejoice in the power you display in weakness.

"My grace is sufficient for you, for power is made perfect in weakness."
2 Cor 12:9

Christ Died for All

2 CORINTHIANS 5:14-21 *14For the love of Christ urges us on, because we are convinced that one has died for all; therefore all have died. 15And he died for all, so that those who live might live no longer for themselves, but for him who died and was raised for them.*

16From now on, therefore, we regard no one from a human point of view; even though we once knew Christ from a human point of view, we know him no longer in that way. 17So if anyone is in Christ, there is a new creation: everything old has passed away; see, everything has become new! 18All this is from God, who reconciled us to himself through Christ, and has given us the ministry of reconciliation; 19that is, in Christ God was reconciling the world to himself, not counting their trespasses against them, and entrusting the message of reconciliation to us. 20So we are ambassadors for Christ, since God is making his appeal through us; we entreat you on behalf of Christ, be reconciled to God. 21For our sake he made him to be sin who knew no sin, so that in him we might become the righteousness of God.

2 CORINTHIANS 12:5-10 *5On behalf of such a one I will boast, but on my own behalf I will not boast, except of my weaknesses. 6But if I wish to boast, I will not be a fool, for I will be speaking the truth. But I refrain from it, so that no one*

may think better of me than what is seen in me or heard from me, ⁷even consid-
ering the exceptional character of the revelations. Therefore, to keep me from
being too elated, a thorn was given me in the flesh, a messenger of Satan to tor-
ment me, to keep me from being too elated. ⁸Three times I appealed to the Lord
about this, that it would leave me, ⁹but he said to me, "My grace is sufficient for
you, for power is made perfect in weakness." So, I will boast all the more gladly
of my weaknesses, so that the power of Christ may dwell in me. ¹⁰Therefore I am
content with weaknesses, insults, hardships, persecutions, and calamities for the
sake of Christ; for whenever I am weak, then I am strong.

In his second letter to the Corinthians, Paul writes about the significance of Christ's cross for his own ministry and for the Christian life. The motivation for Paul's mission is the "love of Christ," a love that was revealed in that Christ "died for all" (5:14–15). This sacrificial love gives Paul a new approach to life: he lives no longer with the values of the world (5:16) but as "a new creation" (5:17). For us, too, an appreciation of Christ crucified turns the values of the world upside down and allows us to live anew.

Because of Christ's sacrifice, the relationship between humanity and God is dramatically different: we have been reconciled to God through Christ (5:18). Objectively, the moment of reconciliation was the moment of the cross—Jesus' death and resurrection. Subjectively, the process of reconciliation is our acceptance in faith of the message of the cross. Through the cross God ceases to count our trespasses against us and reconciles us to himself (5:19); through our acceptance of that gift, we are "reconciled to God" (5:20).

In order to explain the effects of the cross, Paul uses the sacrificial language of the Old Testament. In the sin offering described in Leviticus, the sinner identifies with the animal victim of a sacrifice, so that when the victim is sacrificed, the sinner in effect dies with it. The blood of the victim sprinkled on the altar signifies giving the life to God. Jesus became the atoning sacrifice for humanity; through his death "all have died" (5:14). But through his blood shed on the cross, we have been reconciled to God so that we might live for Christ (5:15). Like the Suffering Servant on whom God laid the iniquity of us all (Isa 53:6), making his life "an offering for sin" (Isa 53:10), Jesus bore our sin on the cross. He "who knew no sin" was made "to be sin" for us (5:21), dying, as our substitute, for sin.

Later in this same letter, Paul speaks personally about his own limitations and sufferings. The test of an authentic mediator or ambassador for Christ is the extent to which he manifests Christ's sacrificial love. How Jesus died is how we must live. So Paul says that he gladly boasts in his weaknesses, because God's grace works in him only when he acknowledges his weakness (12:5, 9). Paul describes his affliction as "a thorn in the flesh" (12:7). It is uncertain whether this suffering refers to a physical illness, a disability, a temptation, or a persecutor. The lesson in Paul's suffering is this: Christ's power is manifested most fully and obviously when we are weak (12:9). Paul boasts in his weaknesses so that the power of Christ may dwell in him.

Reflection and discussion

• What are the old things that have passed away because I have died with Christ? What are the new things that have come to me because of the cross of Christ (5:17)?

• Is our reconciliation with God our work or God's work (5:18-19)? What is our role in this work of reconciliation (5:19-20)?

• Why didn't God just take Paul's "thorn" away after Paul pleaded with him (12:7–9)?

• It is impossible to teach others when they think they know it all or can do everything themselves. Why is it important that we acknowledge our weakness before Christ can work with his grace and power in us?

• When have I experienced that Christ can work better in my weakness than in my strength?

Prayer

Eternal Redeemer, you have reconciled me to God through your cross. Teach me to accept the message of your cross, boast in my weaknesses, endure my suffering, and give you the glory in all things.

We know that our old self was crucified with him so that the body of sin might be destroyed, and we might no longer be enslaved to sin. Rom 6:6

Baptized into the Death of Christ

ROMANS 3:21-26 *²¹But now, apart from law, the righteousness of God has been disclosed, and is attested by the law and the prophets, ²²the righteousness of God through faith in Jesus Christ for all who believe. For there is no distinction, ²³since all have sinned and fall short of the glory of God; ²⁴they are now justified by his grace as a gift, through the redemption that is in Christ Jesus, ²⁵whom God put forward as a sacrifice of atonement by his blood, effective through faith. He did this to show his righteousness, because in his divine forbearance he had passed over the sins previously committed; ²⁶it was to prove at the present time that he himself is righteous and that he justifies the one who has faith in Jesus.*

ROMANS 6:3-11 *³Do you not know that all of us who have been baptized into Christ Jesus were baptized into his death? ⁴Therefore we have been buried with him by baptism into death, so that, just as Christ was raised from the dead by the glory of the Father, so we too might walk in newness of life.*

⁵For if we have been united with him in a death like his, we will certainly be united with him in a resurrection like his. ⁶We know that our old self was crucified with him so that the body of sin might be destroyed, and we might no longer be enslaved to sin. ⁷For whoever has died is freed from sin. ⁸But if we have died with Christ, we believe that we will also live with him. ⁹We know that Christ, being raised from the dead, will never die again; death no longer has dominion over him. ¹⁰The death he died, he died to sin, once for all; but the life he lives, he lives to God. ¹¹So you also must consider yourselves dead to sin and alive to God in Christ Jesus.

T he "righteousness of God" is God's solution to the separation between God and humanity as the result of human rebellion and sinfulness. God's righteousness refers to the action God took to bring separated humanity into a right relationship with himself. This solution of God was gradually unfolding through the Old Testament, "the law and the prophets" (3:21), which paved the way for it. The repair of the broken relationship between God and humanity was accomplished through the cross of Jesus Christ. This restored relationship with God is not something that people can earn or achieve through their own work; it is a free gift from God, the expression of his grace (3:24). The scope of this gift is universal, since all people have sinned and failed to manifest the glory of God (3:23). As an unearned gift, it need only be accepted through the trusting relationship of "faith in Jesus Christ" (3:21, 25–26).

Paul employs three metaphors to describe what God has done for us in the cross of Jesus: justification, redemption, and atonement (3:24–25). Justification is an image drawn from the law courts. It means that God the judge has pronounced a verdict of acquittal, even though the accused was guilty. God has dismissed all accusations against humanity and remitted all punishment. Redemption is an image from the slave market. Slaves in the Roman period could obtain freedom only if someone paid a ransom price, by which they could be redeemed. On the cross, Jesus became the ransom price that secured our freedom. Atonement is an image from the temple. As the priests sprinkled the blood of the sacrificial victim in the Holy of Holies to remove the sins of those for whom the sacrifice was offered, the blood of Christ on the cross becomes a sacrifice of atonement for the consequences of humanity's sin.

What happened to Jesus on the cross happens to believers in baptism. Through baptism "into Christ Jesus" (6:3) believers become completely identified with Christ and personally united with his death and resurrection. This dying and rising with Christ transforms our very being, so that "we too might walk in newness of life" (6:4). Baptism is a crucifixion of our earthbound,

Adam-like "old self" (6:6), so that our sinful self no longer lives and sin no longer controls our lives. Instead, we live with Christ (6:8) and we are "alive to God in Christ Jesus" (6:11).

Paul envisions our dying with Christ and living in him as a step-by-step, daily movement toward Christ-likeness. Objectively we die and rise with Christ at the moment of baptism, but in living out our baptism we conform our lives more and more to the pattern of his dying and rising. The new life of baptism requires a continual deepening of faith which leads to an ever increasing awareness of this union with Christ. Dying with Christ and living with and for him is a daily challenge and privilege, and the Holy Spirit gives us new vitality to live this new life.

Reflection and discussion

• How do each of Paul's three metaphors describe the effects of the cross?

• What is the relationship of the cross to Christian baptism?

Prayer

Crucified and Risen Lord, help me to grasp what being crucified with you means. Free me from my self-centered existence and my sin-prone life. Guide me as I think of myself as dead to sin and newly alive in you.

May I never boast of anything except the cross of our Lord Jesus Christ, by which the world has been crucified to me, and I to the world. Gal 6:14

Crucified with Christ

GALATIANS 2:19-21 ¹⁹*For through the law I died to the law, so that I might live to God. I have been crucified with Christ;* ²⁰*and it is no longer I who live, but it is Christ who lives in me. And the life I now live in the flesh I live by faith in the Son of God, who loved me and gave himself for me.* ²¹*I do not nullify the grace of God; for if justification comes through the law, then Christ died for nothing.*

GALATIANS 3:10-14 ¹⁰*For all who rely on the works of the law are under a curse; for it is written, "Cursed is everyone who does not observe and obey all the things written in the book of the law."* ¹¹*Now it is evident that no one is justified before God by the law; for "The one who is righteous will live by faith."* ¹²*But the law does not rest on faith; on the contrary, "Whoever does the works of the law will live by them."* ¹³*Christ redeemed us from the curse of the law by becoming a curse for us—for it is written, "Cursed is everyone who hangs on a tree"—* ¹⁴*in order that in Christ Jesus the blessing of Abraham might come to the Gentiles, so that we might receive the promise of the Spirit through faith.*

GALATIANS 6:11-17 ¹¹*See what large letters I make when I am writing in my own hand!* ¹²*It is those who want to make a good showing in the flesh that try to compel you to be circumcised—only that they may not be persecuted for* *the cross of Christ. ¹³Even the circumcised do not themselves obey the law, but they want you to be circumcised so that they may boast about your flesh. ¹⁴May I never boast of anything except the cross of our Lord Jesus Christ, by which the world has been crucified to me, and I to the world. ¹⁵For neither circumcision nor uncircumcision is anything; but a new creation is everything! ¹⁶As for those who will follow this rule—peace be upon them, and mercy, and upon the Israel of God. ¹⁷From now on, let no one make trouble for me; for I carry the marks of Jesus branded on my body.*

The crucifixion of Jesus is not only the most crucial event of history, it is also a present experience for believers. Paul says, "I have been crucified with Christ" (2:19). The verb is in the Greek perfect tense, indicating an action that began in the past and continues into the present. Crucifixion with Christ is the daily cruciform existence of the Christian. It means conforming one's life to that of Christ, being incorporated into his way of living and dying. That is why Paul can also say, "It is no longer I who live, but it is Christ who lives in me" (2:20). Being crucified with Christ and letting him live in the believer means taking on his vision of life, his concern for the outcast, his passion for justice, his trust in the Father, his fidelity to the call, and accepting the pain and suffering that comes with such a life.

Paul then explains another meaning of Christ's cross by citing two passages from Deuteronomy describing "curses." The first says that those who do not obey all the laws written in the Torah are under a curse (3:10; Deut 27:26); the second says that anyone hung on a tree is under a curse (3:13; Deut 21:23). All people including Paul have lived under the first curse since trying to follow the many prescriptions of the law creates enslavement. Yet on the cross Christ redeemed us from the curse of the law by becoming a curse for us and embodying our curse as he hung upon the wood of the tree. Rather than live by the law (3:12), we can now live by faith (3:11), which brings about an inner transformation and unites our lives to Christ.

The concluding verses of Paul's letter are written in his own handwriting, rather than dictated to a secretary as was the rest of the letter (6:11). These verses are a summary of the main points of his letter and he writes with "large letters" for greater emphasis. His primary point is that the "cross of our Lord Jesus Christ" (6:12, 14) is the way to salvation for all. Paul states that he can no longer boast of his circumcision which is the ancient sign of his Jewish heritage, and he boldly challenges those who demanded that the Gentiles be circumcised in order to follow Christ. Everything about Paul's former way of life has been made relative in light of the supreme gift of Christ's redemptive suffering and death. His only boast is the cross (6:14).

Since crucifixion was used by the Romans against Jews involved in uprisings, the Jews came to see the cross as an instrument of torture and oppression. For a Jew of the first century to "boast" about a cross was like a Jew of today boasting about a gas chamber. It seemed utterly absurd. Yet, for Paul, he knew he could boast in the cross because he had found ultimate meaning in its power. He no longer follows the standards and enticements of the world. He is now subject to the authority of Christ, whose cross has brought about a "new creation" (6:15)—a new existence where the standards of the world are reversed and hostility and division between people no longer reign.

Paul concludes by stating that he bears the marks (stigmata, in Greek) of Jesus on his body (6:17). This Greek word originally referred to the tattoo marks or brands given to slaves to indicate who owned them. Paul's marks are the physical injuries and emotional scars he acquired as a result of his suffering for the sake of Christ: beatings, imprisonments, stoning, and shipwrecks (2 Cor 11:23–27). These marks are the evidence that he has been "crucified with Christ" (2:19).

Reflection and discussion

• What does being "crucified with Christ" (2:19) mean practically for me?

• What is the difference between living by the law and living by faith (3:11–12)?

• What aspects of my life do I boast about? What reason do I have to boast of the cross (6:14)?

• What does Paul mean when he says "a new creation is everything!" (6:15)?

• What are the marks, wounds, and scars I have acquired as a result of following Christ (6:17)?

Prayer

Jesus, by your holy cross you have redeemed the world. Help me to renounce and leave behind all that is useless or hostile to the goal of my life. May the marks on my body identify me as your possession.

In Christ Jesus you who once were far off have been brought near
by the blood of Christ. Eph 2:13

Reconciled by the Blood of Christ

EPHESIANS 2:11-22 [11] *So then, remember that at one time you Gentiles by birth, called 'the uncircumcision' by those who are called 'the circumcision'—a physical circumcision made in the flesh by human hands—* [12] *remember that you were at that time without Christ, being aliens from the commonwealth of Israel, and strangers to the covenants of promise, having no hope and without God in the world.* [13] *But now in Christ Jesus you who once were far off have been brought near by the blood of Christ.* [14] *For he is our peace; in his flesh he has made both groups into one and has broken down the dividing wall, that is, the hostility between us.* [15] *He has abolished the law with its commandments and ordinances, so that he might create in himself one new humanity in place of the two, thus making peace,* [16] *and might reconcile both groups to God in one body through the cross, thus putting to death that hostility through it.* [17] *So he came and proclaimed peace to you who were far off and peace to those who were near;* [18] *for through him both of us have access in one Spirit to the Father.* [19] *So then you are no longer strangers and aliens, but you are citizens with the saints and also members of the household of God,* [20] *built upon the foundation of the apostles and prophets, with Christ Jesus himself as the cornerstone.* [21] *In him the whole structure is joined* *together and grows into a holy temple in the Lord;* [22]*in whom you also are built together spiritually into a dwelling-place for God.*

Reconciliation is another of the many ways that Paul describes the effects of the cross on the relationship between God and human beings. Reconciliation is overcoming alienation and healing broken relationships by ending the causes of division. In earlier letters Paul wrote about the vertical reconciliation of God and humanity made possible through the cross. Here he writes about the horizontal reconciliation of the Jews and Gentiles, their hostility ended by the cross (verse 16). The two divided ethnic groups of early Christianity are brought together in Christ to create "one new humanity," bringing about "peace" where there was only hostility (verse 15).

Paul reminds the Gentiles, called "the uncircumcision" by Jews, that they have had the most to gain. The Jews were the ones who had a long history of covenant relationship with God and from whom the Messiah had come. The Gentiles who were without Christ, aliens from Israel, strangers to the covenant of promise, and without hope (verse 12) are now in Christ, fellow-citizens with the saints, members of God's household (verse 19). The cross has cancelled all their disadvantages. There is no room for any sense of superiority and inferiority in the church on the basis of ethnic background or any other dividing line that alienates people from one another.

Christ has united all believers in himself by breaking down "the dividing wall" (verse 14). This barrier might allude to the wall that prevented the Gentiles from entering the inner courts of the Jerusalem temple. This fence of separation was accompanied by inscriptions warning the Gentiles of deadly consequences if they crossed the line. But the wall at the temple was only symbolic of the higher ideological barrier created by the religious laws of the Jews, including circumcision, dietary laws, and a host of other prescriptions that in effect separated Jews and Gentiles from any social or religious contact with one another. Paul says that Christ has "abolished the law with its commandments and ordinances," thus reconciling both groups and creating peace (verse 15). While not doing away with the moral law, Christ removed the condemnation for breaking it and he nullified the importance of the ceremonial and dietary laws. The cross became the sign that unites all people into a new humanity and offers access to God for all.

The letter makes clear that the message of the cross led not only to personal salvation but also to social transformation. Divisions between people create a desperate need for unity today. The social divide between rich and poor; the industrial divide between owners and labor; the gender divide between men and women; the generational divide between youth and seniors; the racial divide between white and black; ethnic, political, and religious divisions—everywhere there is alienation and hostility between people. The need for reconciliation between peoples is high on the world's agenda. Discipleship challenges us to be healers and reconcilers, recognizing that the new humanity created by the cross of Jesus is a reality still to be established among us.

Reflection and discussion

• What are the divisions between people that most impact my life? Why is reconciliation no easy goal to achieve?

• What is the difference between creative tension, healthy competition, and differences of opinion, on the one hand, and destructive division and hostile alienation, on the other?

• Why is it necessary that the initiative for reconciliation come first from God? Why is it necessary that we receive from God the power to forgive?

• In what ways can the cross lead to social transformation?

• In what ways is the new temple (verses 19-22) different from the temple that Jesus cleansed in Jerusalem?

Prayer

Wounded Healer, you have reconciled all people through the blood of your cross. Heal the divisions between me and other people and make me a minister of reconciliation in the world today.

I am now rejoicing in my sufferings for your sake, and in my flesh
I am completing what is lacking in Christ's afflictions
for the sake of his body, that is, the church. Col 1:24

Peace through the Blood of the Cross

COLOSSIANS 1:19-24 [19]*For in him all the fullness of God was pleased to dwell,* [20]*and through him God was pleased to reconcile to himself all things, whether on earth or in heaven, by making peace through the blood of his cross.*

[21]*And you who were once estranged and hostile in mind, doing evil deeds,* [22]*he has now reconciled in his fleshly body through death, so as to present you holy and blameless and irreproachable before him—* [23]*provided that you continue securely established and steadfast in the faith, without shifting from the hope promised by the gospel that you heard, which has been proclaimed to every creature under heaven. I, Paul, became a servant of this gospel.*

[24]*I am now rejoicing in my sufferings for your sake, and in my flesh I am completing what is lacking in Christ's afflictions for the sake of his body, that is, the church.*

COLOSSIANS 2:8-15 [8]*See to it that no one takes you captive through philosophy and empty deceit, according to human tradition, according to the elemental spirits of the universe, and not according to Christ.* [9]*For in him the whole* *fullness of deity dwells bodily, ¹⁰and you have come to fullness in him, who is the head of every ruler and authority. ¹¹In him also you were circumcised with a spiritual circumcision, by putting off the body of the flesh in the circumcision of Christ; ¹²when you were buried with him in baptism, you were also raised with him through faith in the power of God, who raised him from the dead. ¹³And when you were dead in trespasses and the uncircumcision of your flesh, God made you alive together with him, when he forgave us all our trespasses, ¹⁴erasing the record that stood against us with its legal demands. He set this aside, nailing it to the cross. ¹⁵He disarmed the rulers and authorities and made a public example of them, triumphing over them in it.*

In the letter to the Ephesians, Paul spoke of the cross reconciling Jews and Gentiles in a new humanity. In this letter to the Colossians, he speaks about the cross reconciling to God "all things, whether on earth or in heaven" (1:20). Since it seems that human sin has disrupted the relationship between God and all creation, creating fractures and alienation (Gen 3:17-19), reconciling "all things" means that the whole universe can be restored to its original wholeness and peace with God. Because in Christ dwells "all the fullness of God" (1:19; 2:9), there are no limits to the atoning power of "the blood of his cross." Christ's crucifixion brings about personal, ethnic, and cosmic reconciliation. It is the one act which brings all of creation into restored peace and harmony with its Creator.

The cross represents a great cosmic drama in which God fights against and triumphs over the powers of evil in the world. The conflict is played out in the life, death, and resurrection of Christ. Anyone who had seen Jesus die would consider the cross a tragedy. Yet, the early Christians claimed that the cross was a triumphant victory. Though hostile forces in the world seek to keep us captive (2:8, 13), Christ triumphed over them, and like a victorious king bringing his disgraced foes into the city, he defeated, disarmed, and humiliated them (2:15).

Paul urges the Colossians to trust in Christ alone and his supreme achievement on the cross. Because only in him dwells the "whole fullness of deity" in bodily form (2:9), he alone can bring about the "fullness" of every person (2:10). Paul uses the Jewish language of circumcision and the Christian language of baptism to describe the incorporation of believers into Christ. As eight-day-old Jewish boys were incorporated into the covenant of Israel through the rite of circumcision, Christians experience a more radical "spiritual circumcision" (2:11) as their initiation into the new covenant. This "circumcision of Christ" is the cutting off of the sinful nature dominated by selfish attachments and alienation from God, a spiritual circumcision accomplished through the sacrifice of Christ on the cross. The rite of the new covenant is Christian baptism. The one who is dead in sin and in an "uncircumcised" state (2:13) is buried with Christ in the waters of baptism and rises with Christ through faith in God's power (2:12). In the believer's new life with Christ, sin is completely forgiven and the record of sin's debt to God is "nailed to the cross" and cancelled (2:14).

The political and religious powers of the times combined with the supernatural powers of evil to insure Christ's tragic and humiliating death on the cross. Yet by submitting to these powers, the crucified Messiah triumphed over them. By the power of God, the cross became the chariot on which the victor rode in triumphant procession, to the humiliation of the defeated enemies (2:15). Henceforth all human suffering could be united with that of Christ and become the means to victorious life. Because Paul was so united with the death and resurrection of Christ, he could claim that his own sufferings were united with the Redeemer's afflictions and continue the effects of his death in the world (1:24). Indeed, our own pains and defeats, when joined with the cross of Christ, are vicarious offerings directed toward the ongoing redemption of Christ's body, the church.

Reflection and discussion

• What are the powers, rulers, and authorities that seek to take us captive and produce evil in human society?

• How does the cross help believers who are living in fear and oppressed by forces that seem too strong for them?

• Why does Paul rejoice in his suffering (1:24)? Have I ever found reason to rejoice in my suffering as it became a benefit for the life of others?

• How is Christian baptism like a spiritual circumcision? In what ways has my baptism united me to the life of Christ?

Prayer

Conquering Lord, though your cross seems to be a tragic defeat, it is in truth the sign of triumphant victory. Banish my fears and conquer my oppressors through your cross and help me to trust in its supreme achievement.

SUGGESTIONS FOR FACILITATORS, GROUP SESSION 5

1. Welcome group members and ask if anyone has any questions, announcements, or requests.

2. You may want to pray this prayer as a group:

Lord Jesus, we rejoice in the wondrous gift of the cross. Through the letters of Paul, we realize that the Scriptures offer us an incredible number of ways to understand the meaning of your cross. It is God's victory over the powers of evil, our atoning sacrifice, our acquittal from the charges against us, our ransom from eternal slavery, our dying and rising with Christ. Your cross inspires us to live a life for others, gives us hope in the midst of suffering, and enables us to trust in your great victory over the temporary powers of this world. Help us to embrace your cross and make us instruments of reconciliation in the world.

3. Ask one or more of the following questions:
   • What insight from Paul's letters most inspired you from this week's study?
   • What new understanding of the cross did you acquire this week?

4. Discuss lessons 19 through 24. Choose one or more of the questions for reflection and discussion from each lesson to talk over as a group.

5. Ask the group members to name one thing they have most appreciated about the way the group has worked during this Bible study. Ask group members to discuss any changes they might suggest in the way the group works in future studies.

6. Invite group members to complete lessons 25 through 30 on their own during the six days before the next meeting. They should write out their own answers to the questions as preparation for next week's session.

7. Ask the group how this study is affecting the way they look upon the crosses and crucifixes in their churches and homes.

8. Conclude by praying aloud together the prayer at the end of one of the lessons discussed. You may want to end the prayer by asking members to voice prayers of thanksgiving.

He humbled himself and became obedient to the point of death —even death on a cross. Phil 2:8

Divine Humility on the Cross

PHILIPPIANS 2:5-11 *⁵Let the same mind be in you that was in Christ Jesus,*
⁶who, though he was in the form of God,
  did not regard equality with God
  as something to be exploited,
⁷but emptied himself,
  taking the form of a slave,
  being born in human likeness.
And being found in human form,
  ⁸he humbled himself
  and became obedient to the point of death—
  even death on a cross.

⁹Therefore God also highly exalted him
  and gave him the name
  that is above every name,
¹⁰so that at the name of Jesus
  every knee should bend,

> *in heaven and on earth and under the earth,*
> [11]*and every tongue should confess*
> *that Jesus Christ is Lord,*
> *to the glory of God the Father.*

PHILIPPIANS 3:10-11 [10]*I want to know Christ and the power of his resurrection and the sharing of his sufferings by becoming like him in his death,* [11]*if somehow I may attain the resurrection from the dead.*

This early Christian hymn summarizes the mystery of the cross. The first half of the hymn (2:6-8) expresses the tragedy of the cross; the second half (2:9-11) the triumph of the cross. The hymn was probably sung at Christian baptisms in which one went under the water to die with Christ and came out of the water to rise with him.

Though Jesus shared the very essence of God, he did not treat his equality with God as an occasion for self-exaltation (2:6). Rather, he displayed his divine nature through self-humiliation. He humbled himself in taking on a human nature (2:7), then he humbled himself further by accepting death. Finally it was in the manner of his death—death on a cross (2:8)—that the rock bottom of humiliation was reached. No experience could be more unspeakably horrible or loathsomely degrading than death on a cross.

Yet, because Jesus descended to the lowest depth, God exalted him to the highest summit (2:9). This great reversal of Christ's humiliation supremely illustrates his own words: "All who humble themselves will be exalted" (Matt 23:12). The humble slave nailed to the cross has been given the name above all names—Jesus is Lord (2:11).

Paul urges his readers: "Let the same mind be in you that was in Christ Jesus" (2:5). When we have taken on the humility and the servant attitude of Christ, we are able to imitate him in our relationships with one another. The crucified Lord is the model for our lives. His saving act on the cross empowers us to live differently, as servants of one another and as people destined for eternal life with him.

At the pivotal point of Paul's letter, he says that his greatest desire is "to know Christ" (3:10). Knowing Christ, for Paul, means to experience Christ more personally and fully. Because in Christ is an inexhaustible fullness, there is always more to know of him. Paul realizes that the heart of knowing Christ is sharing "the power of his resurrection" and the "sharing of his suffering." The power of the resurrection is what gave Paul the strength and grace to carry on his remarkable ministry for Christ and what enables every believer to live a new kind of life. Paul's sharing in Christ's suffering is well documented in his letters, a sharing in the physical and emotional hardships of discipleship with the scars to prove it. Yet, the cross put all of Paul's suffering in a different light. Christ's sufferings enabled Paul to interpret his own, and his own sufferings enabled him to interpret Christ's. Suffering, for Paul, was not a pointless struggle to be faced with gloomy stoicism and a stiff upper lip. Suffering with Christ in the power of the resurrection enabled him to accept trials with strength, courage, and even joy.

"Becoming like Christ in his death" was, for Paul, a matter of present experience, a daily dying with Christ, as well as an anticipation of his own bodily death, which he sensed would take the form of martyrdom for Christ. He knew that dying with Christ was the indispensable condition of "attaining the resurrection from the dead" (3:11). All disciples who unite their sufferings with Christ in self-giving and live in the power of his resurrection day by day can look forward with confident hope to the final resurrection. Then we will be fully transformed into his likeness and know him completely.

Reflection and discussion

• In what ways does Christian baptism express the tragedy and the triumph of the cross?

• In what ways did the divine Christ humble himself?

• How is the cross not only past history but present reality for Christians?

• What does it mean practically for me to humble myself like Christ?

• What does "to know Christ" (3:10) mean? In what ways can I come to know Christ?

Prayer

Crucified Lord, I want to know you more fully each day. Help me to imitate your humility, share in your sufferings, and know the power of your resurrection.

It is by God's will that we have been sanctified through the offering of the body of Jesus Christ once for all. Heb 10:10

Christ's Sacrifice Once for All

HEBREWS 10:1-25 ¹*Since the law has only a shadow of the good things to come and not the true form of these realities, it can never, by the same sacrifices that are continually offered year after year, make perfect those who approach. ²Otherwise, would they not have ceased being offered, since the worshipers, cleansed once for all, would no longer have any consciousness of sin? ³But in these sacrifices there is a reminder of sin year after year. ⁴For it is impossible for the blood of bulls and goats to take away sins. ⁵Consequently, when Christ came into the world, he said,*

> *"Sacrifices and offerings you have not desired,*
>   *but a body you have prepared for me;*
> ⁶*in burnt offerings and sin offerings*
>   *you have taken no pleasure.*
> ⁷*Then I said, 'See, God, I have come to do your will, O God'*
>   *(in the scroll of the book it is written of me)."*

⁸*When he said above, "You have neither desired nor taken pleasure in sacrifices and offerings and burnt offerings and sin offerings" (these are offered according to the law), ⁹then he added, "See, I have come to do your will." He abolishes the*

first in order to establish the second. [10] *And it is by God's will that we have been sanctified through the offering of the body of Jesus Christ once for all.*

[11] *And every priest stands day after day at his service, offering again and again the same sacrifices that can never take away sins.* [12] *But when Christ had offered for all time a single sacrifice for sins, "he sat down at the right hand of God,"* [13] *and since then has been waiting "until his enemies would be made a footstool for his feet."* [14] *For by a single offering he has perfected for all time those who are sanctified.* [15] *And the Holy Spirit also testifies to us, for after saying,*

[16] *"This is the covenant that I will make with them*
after those days, says the Lord:
I will put my laws in their hearts,
and I will write them on their minds,"
[17] *he also adds,*
"I will remember their sins and their lawless deeds no more."
[18] *Where there is forgiveness of these, there is no longer any offering for sin.*

[19] *Therefore, my friends, since we have confidence to enter the sanctuary by the blood of Jesus,* [20] *by the new and living way that he opened for us through the curtain (that is, through his flesh),* [21] *and since we have a great priest over the house of God,* [22] *let us approach with a true heart in full assurance of faith, with our hearts sprinkled clean from an evil conscience and our bodies washed with pure water.* [23] *Let us hold fast to the confession of our hope without wavering, for he who has promised is faithful.* [24] *And let us consider how to provoke one another to love and good deeds,* [25] *not neglecting to meet together, as is the habit of some, but encouraging one another, and all the more as you see the Day approaching.*

T he entire letter to the Hebrews explains the cross of Christ through terminology familiar from the Old Testament: the cross is the ultimate sacrifice, offered by the perfect high priest, establishing a new covenant. This passage summarizes the teachings of the letter, demonstrating that the sacrificial system of the old law was "only a shadow" of the "true form" found in Christ's cross (verse 1).

The first verses offer a critique of the temple sacrifices, especially those made on the Day of Atonement. Those same sacrifices had to be "continually offered year after year." The endless repetition of sacrifices pointed to their inadequacy in fulfilling their purpose. They did not truly transform people and absolve their interior consciences, but were, rather, an annual reminder of sin, prolonging the agony of guilt (verses 2-3). In addition, "the blood of bulls and goats" could not truly take away sin, for brute animals, without a mind, will, and consciousness, could never substitute for human beings (verse 4). Sinful people need a willing substitute to cleanse them through sacrifice.

The sacrifice of Christ was truly effective because his life was one of total self-giving and obedience (verses 5-9). Under the old covenant, people often offered sacrifice without the corresponding obedience to God's commands. But that deficiency was settled once and for all in Jesus who fulfilled the ideal life set out in Psalm 40:6-8. A life of doing God's will was more pleasing to God than all the offerings and sacrifices of the old covenant. The total self-offering of Jesus to the will of the Father, climaxing in his crucifixion, introduced an unprecedented and ideal form of sacrifice, the offering of the new humanity. This is a sacrifice that was offered "once for all" (verse 10). Because it truly sanctifies us, there is no need for a daily or even yearly offering. The entire life of the church, with its Eucharist and sacraments, makes present in time the one sacrifice of Christ. The here and now experience of God's grace is possible only because of the then and there offering of Jesus Christ.

In addition to being the ultimate sacrifice, Jesus is also the perfect high priest who establishes the new covenant. The priests of the former covenant were compelled to offer sacrifices day after day. Yet their never-ending task could never "take away sins" (verse 11). Their offerings only pointed to Jesus, the new high priest, whose single offering perfected us for all time (verse 14). As the priestly mediator between God and humanity, Christ became our ideal representative before God through his self-offering experienced through humility, weakness. and suffering. Though his sacrifice is complete, his priestly intercession continues from his exalted place in heaven (verse 12), offering salvation to all who look to him.

The cross is the sacrifice that not only atones for sins but also inaugurates the new covenant. This is a covenant that brings about a decisive and inward change in people's lives. God's law will no longer be an external code, but an inner law written in the minds and hearts of God's people (verse 16). Truly forgiven, freed from perpetually nagging feelings of shame and guilt, we have confidence to approach God (verses 17-19). What had previously been the unique privilege of the high priest one day in the year, entry into the presence of God, is now the privilege of every member of the community of faith. We have direct access to God because the curtain shielding the Holy of Holies has been parted through the death of Jesus on the cross (verse 20). His sacrificial blood has opened for us "the new and living way," beckoning us to come in with him to the presence of God. This spiritualized language of the ancient temple expresses the new confidence we have before God. Assured of our forgiveness, cleansed of guilt, we can worship our God in freedom and in truth, united with him in an awesome intimacy.

Reflection and discussion

• What heroic or generous sacrifices for others have most inspired me? What made these selfless deeds to be sacrifices?

• What is it about Christ that makes his work so much more effective than the ancient system of sacrifices?

• What are the practical consequences of my invitation to go behind the curtain into God's presence (verses 19-20)?

• In what way does the "once for all" sacrifice of Christ continue to be made present through time?

• What is so "new" about the new covenant?

• How can trust and confidence in Christ's cross free me from nagging feelings of shame and guilt?

Prayer

Merciful Lord, you are both the priest and the victim for the once-and-for-all sacrifice of the cross. Assure me that I am truly forgiven and free my conscience from the guilt of sin. Help me to live in the new covenant with trust and confidence.

Let us run with perseverance the race that is set before us, looking to Jesus the pioneer and perfecter of our faith, who endured the cross. Heb 12:1-2

Persevere through Trials and Hardships

HEBREWS 12:1-13 ¹*Therefore, since we are surrounded by so great a cloud of witnesses, let us also lay aside every weight and the sin that clings so closely, and let us run with perseverance the race that is set before us, ²looking to Jesus the pioneer and perfecter of our faith, who for the sake of the joy that was set before him endured the cross, disregarding its shame, and has taken his seat at the right hand of the throne of God.*

³Consider him who endured such hostility against himself from sinners, so that you may not grow weary or lose heart. ⁴In your struggle against sin you have not yet resisted to the point of shedding your blood. ⁵And you have forgotten the exhortation that addresses you as children—

"My child, do not regard lightly the discipline of the Lord,
or lose heart when you are punished by him;
⁶for the Lord disciplines those whom he loves,
and chastises every child whom he accepts."

⁷Endure trials for the sake of discipline. God is treating you as children; for what child is there whom a parent does not discipline? ⁸If you do not have that discipline in which all children share, then you are illegitimate and not his children.

⁹Moreover, we had human parents to discipline us, and we respected them. Should we not be even more willing to be subject to the Father of spirits and live? ¹⁰For they disciplined us for a short time as seemed best to them, but he disciplines us for our good, in order that we may share his holiness. ¹¹Now, discipline always seems painful rather than pleasant at the time, but later it yields the peaceful fruit of righteousness to those who have been trained by it.

¹²Therefore lift your drooping hands and strengthen your weak knees, ¹³and make straight paths for your feet, so that what is lame may not be put out of joint, but rather be healed.

The author is attempting to help the Christian community make sense out of its suffering—to give a positive meaning to something that is experienced as decidedly negative. Followers of Jesus are to endure their hardships and to persevere through their trials, because there is joy at the end of suffering. The life of a disciple is like a race; we are urged to run toward the goal, fixing our sight on the completion of the race. As runners remove everything that could weigh them down, we must remove from our lives anything that slows us down and hinders us from persevering to the end (verse 1).

In the great stadium of life, we are cheered on by a host of "witnesses" who surround us like a cloud (verse 1), that large group of heroes of faith from the Old Testament enumerated in the previous chapter. They have all run before us, and now they are watching to see how we will perform. But above all, we must keep our eyes fixed on Jesus, who has run the race ahead of us through enduring his cross. He is our leader, the one who perfects our faith, so that we can persevere. As Jesus endured the cross, the disciple is to endure the race (verse 2). Jesus bore the cross because he set his sight on the joyful victory at the end, the resurrection and new life. Many others have done it before us; Jesus has done it; we too can persevere and run the grueling race, looking forward to the victory that follows.

The author describes the trials of a Christian as "discipline" (verse 7). By citing from Proverbs 3:11-12, the author demonstrates that the discipline and chastisement they experience are a mark of God's parental love (verses 5-6). A true parent disciplines his children for their own benefit (verse 10). At the time of trial such discipline seems to be the cause of much pain, but when the discipline is accepted, it brings about joy and peaceful fruits (verse 11).

So "strengthen your drooping hands and your weak knees" (verse 12); the race is on. We are surrounded and encouraged by the whole community of faith, on earth and in eternity. We will not "grow weary and lose heart" (verse 3) if we look to Jesus who carried his cross to the finish line and won the prize of victory. He teaches us how to get a second wind, to keep our eyes on the prize, and never lose sight of the victory that awaits us.

Reflection and discussion

• Who do I know who has run the race of life at the pace I would like to imitate? In what aspect of life am I in danger of growing weary and losing heart?

• Describe the style of discipline that is a mark of loving parenting.

Prayer

Jesus, my leader and perfecter of faith, help me to accept the discipline of suffering. As you endured the cross, help me to persevere in the trials of life so that I may reap the reward you promise me.

He himself bore our sins in his own body on the cross, so that, free from sins, we might live for righteousness. 1 Peter 2:24

Healed by His Wounds

1 PETER 1:17-21 [17]*If you invoke as Father the one who judges all people impartially according to their deeds, live in reverent fear during the time of your exile.* [18]*You know that you were ransomed from the futile ways inherited from your ancestors, not with perishable things like silver or gold,* [19]*but with the precious blood of Christ, like that of a lamb without defect or blemish.* [20]*He was destined before the foundation of the world, but was revealed at the end of the ages for your sake.* [21]*Through him you have come to trust in God, who raised him from the dead and gave him glory, so that your faith and hope are set on God.*

1 PETER 2:21-24 [21]*For to this you have been called, because Christ also suffered for you, leaving you an example, so that you should follow in his steps.*
   [22]*"He committed no sin,*
       and no deceit was found in his mouth."
[23]*When he was abused, he did not return abuse; when he suffered, he did not threaten; but he entrusted himself to the one who judges justly.* [24]*He himself bore our sins in his body on the cross, so that, free from sins, we might live for righteousness; by his wounds you have been healed.*

Peter's first letter refers more to the cross of Jesus than any other New Testament letter. To Peter, the cross forms the framework of discipleship and gives shape to the whole Christian experience. He reflected on it deeply, and finally he embraced it during his own martyrdom by crucifixion.

While we live in exile on the earth, we must live in "reverent fear" of the "one who judges all people impartially." Yet we are able to call upon this just, divine Judge as our "Father" because we have been ransomed by the sacrifice of Christ from the "futile ways" of the past (1:17–18). The cost of establishing such a relationship with God has not been cheap. The metaphor of salvation comes from the ancient culture in which slaves could purchase their freedom with a hefty ransom price. The ransom paid for our freedom is not made with mere silver or gold, but with "the precious blood of Christ," a price that is both inestimable and eternal (1:19). Nor was our ransom a mere afterthought, hastily produced to remedy a human situation that had gone unexpectedly wrong. No, our redemption by Christ was "destined before the foundation of the world" (1:20). His death on the cross was no unfortunate accident, but was the perfect sacrifice prepared by God as the culmination of his eternal plan.

The cross of Christ has rescued us from the prison of futility and enabled us to call God our Father. Meaningless existence has evaporated into a life of ultimate meaning, founded on the eternal plan and purpose of God. Because of the cross we are able to trust in God (1:21). We are now a people of hope, no longer meandering through a pointless wilderness, but journeying through the time of our exile with a sense of direction and destiny.

But not only is the crucified Christ our valuable ransom price, he is also our supreme "example" to imitate, our mentor in suffering (2:21). As our ransom, he is the Passover lamb of Exodus; as our example, he is the Suffering Servant of Isaiah. In holding up Jesus as our model, Peter uses descriptive phrases from Isaiah 53. Jesus was the innocent sufferer; though abused and afflicted, he did not retaliate or seek revenge. He was a model of patient endurance, confidently entrusting himself to "the one who judges justly" (2:22–23). As the Suffering Servant, he bore the burden of our sins, so that we might live anew as forgiven and healed people (2:24).

Peter had learned so much since those early days in Galilee when he heard the call of Jesus, "Follow me" (Matt 4:19). At the critical moment of Jesus' arrest, Peter was "following him at a distance" (Matt 26:58). Now at a critical time for the early church, Peter exhorts the suffering community of Jesus' disciples to "follow in his steps" (2:21), in the very footprints of their cross-bearing Lord.

Reflection and discussion

• Which of Peter's insights into the meaning of the cross is most helpful to me?

• What does the example of Jesus teach me about responding to suffering in a healthy way?

• Why is one who has been wounded often the best healer of others?

Prayer

Wounded Healer, help me to be mindful of you in the midst of my suffering. Transform my suffering into a graced encounter with you so that I may experience healing and life.

In this is love, not that we loved God but that he loved us and sent his Son to be the atoning sacrifice for our sins. 1 John 4:10

The Cross Reveals God's Love

1 JOHN 3:16-20 [16]*We know love by this, that he laid down his life for us—and we ought to lay down our lives for one another.* [17]*How does God's love abide in anyone who has the world's goods and sees a brother or sister in need and yet refuses help?*

[18]*Little children, let us love, not in word or speech, but in truth and action.* [19]*And by this we will know that we are from the truth and will reassure our hearts before him* [20]*whenever our hearts condemn us; for God is greater than our hearts, and he knows everything.*

1 JOHN 4:7-14 [7]*Beloved, let us love one another, because love is from God; everyone who loves is born of God and knows God.* [8]*Whoever does not love does not know God, for God is love.* [9]*God's love was revealed among us in this way: God sent his only Son into the world so that we might live through him.* [10]*In this is love, not that we loved God but that he loved us and sent his Son to be the atoning sacrifice for our sins.* [11]*Beloved, since God loved us so much, we also ought to love one another.* [12]*No one has ever seen God; if we love one another, God lives in us, and his love is perfected in us.*

¹³*By this we know that we abide in him and he in us, because he has given us of his Spirit.* ¹⁴*And we have seen and do testify that the Father has sent his Son as the Savior of the world.*

The most remarkable statement in the first letter of John is the revelation of God's essence: "God is love"(4:8). The entire letter might be described as an explanation of this statement. This divine love is not the kind of love that we often see in movies, songs, and popular culture. The Greek word John uses is *agape*, which is the commitment to seek the good of the other.

We know that God is love because of his actions, his self-disclosure in the world. And the highest manifestation of God's love is the cross. We might tend to describe love as a powerful emotion or a comfortable feeling. But God has shown us that the best definition of love is not to be found in words, but in the concrete symbol of the cross. The cross describes love as self-giving: "We know love by this, that he laid down his life for us" (3:16). The cross reveals to us, in the most compelling and undeniable manner, that God is love.

It is a hazard in every age that genuine love deteriorates into sentimentality. The divine love that we have been shown in the cross of Christ is not sentiment. The cross convinces us that the forgiveness we have been given in Christ is not an easy pardon, a cheap grace, a divine shrug that pretends the horrible rift of human sin never happened. Rather, God's love penetrates to the heart, where sin and indifference reside, and deals with the root causes of our separation from God. "He loved us and sent his Son to be the atoning sacrifice for our sins" (4:10). The healing and reconciliation that only true love can create is established through the work of atonement, a process that was prefigured by the blood sacrifices of Israel's ancient Yom Kippur (Day of Atonement) and completed in the self-offering of Christ on the cross.

The cross not only reveals God's love, but it motivates us to manifest God's love through our own lives. Because Christ laid down his life out of love for us, "we ought to lay down our lives for one another" (3:16; 4:11). The love of God should never flow into our lives without also flowing through us to others. To receive God's love and then refuse to share it with others is to turn the living waters of God's love into a stagnant pool. This offering of ourselves for others is done through very concrete actions, like helping "a brother or sister in need" (3:17). Mere words are never enough when it comes to expressing love; true love demands action (3:18).

God's love manifested on the cross is not just a revelation to be admired, but an example to be imitated. Not only is God's love revealed through the sacrificial actions of our lives, but it is "perfected in us" (4:12). The historical manifestation of God's love through the cross of Calvary is continuously consummated in the loving deeds of God's people. When God's love is reproduced in us and expressed in the world today through sacrificial service and love of neighbor, God's love is completed and achieves its full effect.

Reflection and discussion

• Why is the cross a better explanation of God's love than a written definition? When have I needed more than sentiment to express love?

• What types of loving deeds reproduce and express the cross of Christ in the world today?

Prayer

Loving God, the cross is the greatest sign of your love for me. Motivate me to manifest your love in the world and to perfect the work of Christ's cross through offering myself for the good of others in need.

Worthy is the Lamb that was slaughtered to receive power and wealth and wisdom and might and honor and glory and blessing! Rev 5:12

The Slaughtered and Glorified Lamb

REVELATION 5:1-14 ¹ *Then I saw in the right hand of the one seated on the throne a scroll written on the inside and on the back, sealed with seven seals;* ² *and I saw a mighty angel proclaiming with a loud voice, "Who is worthy to open the scroll and break its seals?"* ³ *And no one in heaven or on earth or under the earth was able to open the scroll or to look into it.* ⁴ *And I began to weep bitterly because no one was found worthy to open the scroll or to look into it.* ⁵ *Then one of the elders said to me, "Do not weep. See, the Lion of the tribe of Judah, the Root of David, has conquered, so that he can open the scroll and its seven seals."*

⁶ *Then I saw between the throne and the four living creatures and among the elders a Lamb standing as if it had been slaughtered, having seven horns and seven eyes, which are the seven spirits of God sent out into all the earth.* ⁷ *He went and took the scroll from the right hand of the one who was seated on the throne.* ⁸ *When he had taken the scroll, the four living creatures and the twenty-four elders fell before the Lamb, each holding a harp and golden bowls full of incense, which are the prayers of the saints.* ⁹ *They sing a new song:*

"You are worthy to take the scroll
  and to open its seals,

for you were slaughtered and by your blood you ransomed for God
  saints from every tribe and language and people and nation;
¹⁰*you have made them to be a kingdom and priests serving our God,*
  and they will reign on earth."
¹¹*Then I looked, and I heard the voice of many angels surrounding the throne*
and the living creatures and the elders; they numbered myriads of myriads and
thousands of thousands, ¹²*singing with full voice,*
  "Worthy is the Lamb that was slaughtered
  to receive power and wealth and wisdom and might
  and honor and glory and blessing!"
¹³*Then I heard every creature in heaven and on earth and under the earth and*
in the sea, and all that is in them, singing,
  "To the one seated on the throne and to the Lamb
  be blessing and honor and glory and might
  forever and ever!"
¹⁴*And the four living creatures said, "Amen!" And the elders fell down and worshiped.*

The book of Revelation fittingly concludes the biblical teaching about the tragic and triumphant cross with symbolic drama. The scroll with the seven seals, held in God's right hand, contains the divine plan to redeem the whole of creation and reclaim the fallen world (verse 1). This divine plan, foreshadowed in the Hebrew scriptures, was put into effect through the sacrificial death of Christ. Thus, there is only One who is worthy and able to open this scroll and break its seven seals—the divine Lamb (verses 2-5).

Throughout the book of Revelation the Lamb is the dominant image for the triumph of God's saving plan. This symbolic creature, representing the crucified and glorified Christ, stands in the center of God's throne and receives all the praise of the heavenly multitudes. He is the one who has put God's redemptive plan into effect and who, now enthroned in heaven, will see that it comes to completion.

The Lamb is described as having seven horns, seven eyes, and possessing the seven spirits of God sent throughout the earth (verse 6). Since seven represents completion and perfection, this very non-literal image expresses the all-powerful and all-knowing nature of Christ, and the omnipresence of his Spirit released to accomplish his work in the world. More significantly, the Lamb is described as "standing as if it had been slaughtered" (verse 6). This is no imperial conqueror, but a pathetic and diminutive lamb, bearing the effects of its sacrificial slaughter, yet standing in conquest. Here is the wounded though risen Christ.

The blood of Christ ransomed a great worldwide multitude, "saints from every tribe and language and people and nation" (verse 9). From the nationalism of Israel and the ethnic exclusiveness of Judaism comes a universal people. He who died as a king and a priest now extends his royal and holy reign throughout the world, making all his disciples "a kingdom and priests," reigning on the earth and serving God in the new, universal priesthood (verse 10).

The universality of Christ's victory on the cross calls for a universal response. He is praised by the patriarchs and apostles of old (verse 8), by thousands upon thousands of angels (verse 11), and by "every creature in heaven and on earth and under the earth and in the sea" (verse 13). No part of the created universe is excluded from the redeeming and reconciling power of the cross. All creation sings a new song with full voice, falling down in worship before God and the Lamb.

The cross, which in the eyes of the world looks to be a symbol of defeat, poverty, foolishness, weakness, shame, disgrace, and cursing, has been transformed through the wondrous plan of God into an instrument of "power and wealth and wisdom and might and honor and glory and blessing!" (verse 12). Christ, still bearing the marks of his crucifixion, reigns forever over the world.

Reflection and discussion

• Why is it significant that Christ reigning over the world still bears the wounds of his cross?

• Why is this image of the Lamb such an effective way of summing up the Bible's teaching about the tragic and triumphant cross?

• How will Holy Week and Easter be different for me after this study?

• What is the primaary insight I have gained through this study of the cross?

Prayer

Glorious Christ, you have conquered the powers of darkness and called your people to be a universal kingdom of priests. May we lift high your glorious cross and proclaim your victory to all the world.

SUGGESTIONS FOR FACILITATORS, GROUP SESSION 6

1. Welcome group members and make any final announcements or requests.

2. You may want to pray this prayer as a group:

Crucified Lord, you are the slain and glorified Lamb, the atoning sacrifice for all the world, our wounded healer. You ran the race ahead of us, carrying your cross to the finish line to claim the reward of victory for us. You are worthy to receive our worship forever because through your cross you have saved us and set us free. We lift high your glorious cross, proclaiming to the whole world that you are worthy to receive power and wealth, wisdom and might, honor and glory and blessing.

3. Ask one or more of the following questions:
   • In what way has this study challenged you the most?
   • What words do you think of now when you look upon the cross?

4. Discuss lessons 25 through 30. Choose one or more of the questions for reflection and discussion from each lesson to discuss as a group.

5. Ask the group if they would like to study another book in the Theshold Bible Study series. Discuss the topic and dates, and make a decision among those interested. Ask the group members to suggest people they would like to invite to participate in the next study series.

6. Ask the group to discuss the insights that stand out most from this study over the past six weeks and how the sign of the cross will hold a richer meaning from now on.

7. Conclude by praying aloud the following prayer or another of your own choosing:

Holy Spirit of the crucified Lord, you inspired the sacred writers of the Bible and you have guided our study during these weeks. Continue to deepen our love for the word of God in the holy Scriptures and draw us as disciples to the cross of Christ. Bless us with the sacrificial love of Christ so that we may offer that love to those in need. Bless us with the fire of your love.

Ordering Additional Studies

AVAILABLE TITLES IN THIS SERIES INCLUDE...

Advent Light • Angels of God • Eucharist

The Feasts of Judaism • The Holy Spirit and Spiritual Gifts

Jerusalem, the Holy City • The Lamb and the Beasts

Mysteries of the Rosary • The Names of Jesus

People of the Passion • Pilgrimage in the Footsteps of Jesus

The Resurrection and the Life • The Sacred Heart of Jesus

Stewardship of the Earth • The Tragic and Triumphant Cross

Jesus, the Messianic King (Part 1): Matthew 1–16

Jesus, the Messianic King (Part 2): Matthew 17–28

COMING 2011	COMING 2012
Jesus, the Word Made Flesh (Part 1): John 1–10	Church of the Holy Spirit (Part 1): Acts of the Apostles 1–14
Jesus, the Word Made Flesh (Part 2): John 11–21	Church of the Holy Spirit (Part 2): Acts of the Apostles 15–28
Jesus, the Suffering Servant (Part 1): Mark 1–8	Jesus, the Compassionate Savior (Part 1): Luke 1–11
Jesus, the Suffering Servant (Part 2): Mark 9–16	Jesus, the Compassionate Savior (Part 2): Luke 12–24

To check availability or for a description
of each study, visit our website at
www.ThresholdBibleStudy.com
or call us at **1-800-321-0411**